MONEY GALORE

The Story of the Welsh Pound

Ivor Wynne Jones

Published by

Landmark Publishing Ltd
Ashbourne Hall, Cokayne Ave, Ashbourne, Derbyshire DE6 1EJ England
Tel: (01335) 347349 Fax: (01335) 347303
e-mail: landmark@clara.net
web site: www.landmarkpublishing.co.uk

ISBN 1 84306 084 1

British Library Cataloguing in Publication Data: a catalogue
record for this book is available from the British Library.

Print: Cambrian Printers
Design: Mark Titterton
Cover: James Allsopp

Front cover: Williams's first £1 note.
Title page: 50 New Pence Sterling.
Back cover: Richard Williams 1915-1988.

LANDMARK COLLECTOR'S LIBRARY

MONEY GALORE

THE STORY OF THE WELSH POUND

Ivor Wynne Jones

Landmark Publishing

Contents

Introduction

Old and new currencies

Bracketed translations within the text of obsolete pre-decimal monetary terms, such as £-s-d, would have caused all manner of problems, not least of which would have been the need to explain which alternative "pence" one meant at any given time. All monetary terms are therefore written in their radical value for the date concerned.

Decimalisation of British currency was introduced in 1971, when the replacement pennies, at the rate of 100 to the pound, were described as "new pence" – although the "50 new pence" coin was issued and used from 1969, when its value equated to 120 pence of the currency then in use. In 1982 the legend on this coin was changed to "50 pence". The original "10 new pence" coin was issued in 1968, identical in size to the florin and worth 24 pence. Similarly the original "5 new pence" coin was issued in 1968 to match the shilling coin in size, and worth 12 pence. The first 2p, 1p and ½p coins were also described as "new pence" until the legend on all the new coins was changed in 1982, when the sizes of the larger denominations were reduced. The new halfpenny was last minted in 1984.

Before 1971 the pound divided into a mathematically versatile 240 pence, with 12 pence to a shilling and 20 shillings to the pound. As is explained in the text, the penny was always denoted as "d" for historical reasons. The shilling was denoted by "s" though not as an abbreviation for "shilling" – a point also explained in the text. In addition, the long-obsolete "guinea" was an expression regularly used and universally understood, right up to 1971, one guinea representing one pound plus one shilling, or 21 shillings. Within the pounds, shillings and pence system one guinea could be written as £1/1/-, £1-1s-0d or 21s. The florin coin, an 1848 attempt at decimalisation at ten to the pound, remained in use until 1982, and was worth two shillings or 24 pence until 1971, and 10 new pence until 1982. There was also the half-crown, being an eighth of a pound, and worth two shillings and six pence, denoted as 2/6d. The farthing was last minted in 1956, and was worth a quarter of a pre-decimalisation penny.

Wales, the only gold-producing country in the United Kingdom, is also the only country in the world without its own paper currency, a deficiency Llandudno entrepreneur Richard Williams briefly remedied in 1969, when he printed his own money and fooled the London establishment into endorsing it with the embossed two-penny tax stamp which was then required on all promissory notes other than those of the Bank of England and the authorised issuing banks of Scotland and Northern Ireland.

His activities resulted in the Government's abolition of its 118-years-old stamp duty on 1 February 1971, so as to eliminate the embarrassment of lending authenticity to this somewhat bizarre private enterprise Welsh money. By that time, however, hundreds of Richard Williams's Government-authenticated notes were in circulation, soon to become rare international collectors' items – much to the surprise of their creator, who was aided and abetted by the author.

Although interpreted as an enterprising Welsh nationalist gesture, Williams was apolitical and his money was initially printed as part of his campaign to retrieve £25m and $5b he said was owed by the banks of Britain and the United States, for the use of his magnetic cheque encoding system – the machine-readable numerals printed across the bottom of all our cheques.

Richard Hugh Williams was born at Caernarfon in 1915, eventually to become a clerk with Midland Bank. Returning to the bank after service as a junior officer with the Royal Navy (RNVR) during World War Two, he became absorbed by the concept of modernising the cumbersome labour-intensive manual banking process with electronic equipment. By 1952 he had developed the seeds of today's systems, which he failed to patent. In 1955 he published a book entitled *The Electronic Office,* which concentrated on banking, and in 1957 he and his wife, Eirlys Evangeline (who hailed from Dolgellau), established a family company called Computer Consultants Ltd.

In September 1968 he realised his folly in not having sought a patent for his systems, and began his plot to claim a royalty for use of what he mistakenly believed to be his copyright (one cannot copyright an idea, only its application). The finance panel of the new Welsh Economic Advisory Council (comprising 36 Government-appointed advisers, superseding the 1948-66 Council for Wales & Monmouthshire) was investigating the need for a Bank of Wales, as part of a wider study of facilities required for financing Welsh industry. On 16 September Williams wrote to Harold Wilson, at 10 Downing Street, beginning "Dear Prime Minister..." His letter asked what steps he could take, "without having to blow up any buildings", to ensure the prestigious title "Bank of Wales" would be reserved for use in the best interests of the entire Principality. In practice, as will be demonstrated later, the elusive title "Bank of Wales" has been a poisoned chalice for nearly one-and-a-half centuries.

His letter produced three replies: an acknowledgement from the Prime Minister's office; an ego-boosting letter from the Welsh Office inviting him to set out his views more fully for consideration by the Finance Panel; and a letter from the Board of Trade stating: *"You may rest assured that no company would be registered with the name of Bank of Wales Ltd. unless the Board considered this fully justified."*

Williams's devilish response was to apply to the Board of Trade for registration of a company to be called Prif Trysorfa Cymru Ltd., with a share capital of £100, in one hundred shares, himself holding 51 and his wife the remainder. His memorandum of association, dated 12 October 1968, set out the objects of the company as being: "To promote all interests in Wales". With commendable speed the Assistant Registrar of Companies granted a certificate of incorporation, No. 941507, on 31 October. Not until four months later did the Board of Trade realise they had registered a Welsh name which translates as Chief Treasury of Wales Ltd!

On 1 November Williams's Prif Trysorfa Cymru fired a shot across the bows of the Welsh Office with a letter to Secretary of State George Thomas stating: *"In view of the fact that we have now registered a company which in due course will increase its capital very considerably, and which will then take on the activities which would normally, perhaps, have been undertaken by a Bank of Wales, we feel that any further discussion by you or your colleagues on the formation of a possible Bank of Wales are now unnecessary. I am sure you will like to take the opportunity of wishing our company every success in the future."*

On the same day he wrote to the Prime Minister, saying: *"We trust you will feel pleased at the initiative taken. Initially our company will act as a discount and acceptance house. It will then assume other responsibilities, including those which would normally be undertaken by a Bank of Wales if such an organisation had existed."*

Williams's audacity knew no bounds, for his letter continued: *"The necessary capital is available to us from a number of sources, including the United States of America, but before taking advantage of the offer of additional capital from organisations that have purely commercial interests at heart, we wonder if your Government would care to offer us any capital from its own resources? We regret we cannot afford to delay matters unduly, and therefore we must request a decision, in principle, within the next seven days."*

Stretching the truth a little, he told the Prime Minister: *"Perhaps we should mention for the record that our associate companies have properties and offices in the North Wales Development Area, as well as computer and other equipment, readily available and waiting."* He was referring to his option to buy Marl Hall, near Llandudno, in which to set up a computer college – if he could persuade the Government to give him a grant of £650,000.

A letter was despatched to Sir Leslie O'Brien, Governor of the Bank of England (1966-73), inviting him to become chairman of Williams's Chief Treasury of Wales. With commendable politeness, Sir Leslie replied, on 14 November: *"While nothing is certain in this life, I do not think that there is any prospect of my being able to entertain your kind suggestion that I should accept the Chairmanship of your company. Nevertheless I appreciate the fact that you should have seen fit to invite me to do so."*

Meanwhile, in that October of 1968, Computer Consultants Ltd. began sending monthly invoices to 25 British banks, claiming one penny royalty for every cheque used, with estimates based on clearance figures published in banking journals. The value of the invoices totalled £1,200,000 every month.

So as to emphasise the existence of Prif Trysorfa Cymru, Williams printed bills of exchange, a device going back to the 13th century activities of the immigrant financiers of Lombardy, who set up their money-lending businesses in London. One of the earliest surviving bills of exchange, preserved in the City of London archives, is for 30s, obtained in 1393 by Iorwerth ap Rhys, of North Wales, from Nicholas Luke, a London Lombard, and payable in Venice. By 1968 it was a somewhat old-fashioned but perfectly legitimate means of advancing money. A person seeking an advance of £5 would sign a bill promising to pay the Chief Treasury of Wales five guineas in three months, which would be equal to an annual interest rate of 20%. In theory Williams's company could discount these bills with any financial institution interested in buying them to reap some of the interest. By the end of 1968 Williams was offering books of "payment orders" barely

CERTIFICATE OF INCORPORATION

No. 941507

I hereby certify that

PRIF TRYSORFA CYMRU LIMITED

is this day incorporated under the Companies Acts 1948 to 1967 and that the Company is Limited.

Given under my hand at London the **31st October 1968.**

Assistant Registrar of Companies

C.173

Certificate of incorporation of Prif Trysorfa Cymru, Williams's
"licence to print money."

THE WAY THINGS GET ABOUT.

Young Smith. "THEY SAY THE MIDDLESEX AND JERUSALEM BANK HAS SMASHED."

Old Brown. "BOSH! I HAPPEN TO KNOW THE CONTRARY."

Young Smith. "REALLY? THEN IT MUST BE THE MIDDLESEX AND SOMETHING ELSE; BUT I DO THINK THERE SHOULD BE SOME WAY OF *PUNISHING* THE IDIOTS WHO GO SPREADING THESE REPORTS ABOUT."

distinguishable from cheques, save for an unexplained black patch in the bottom left corner – the fundamental reason for the whole operation, as will be explained later.

These imitation cheques were available to anyone who wished to open an account with his Chief Treasury. Complex though the system might look, it proved as workable as if Williams were running a bank. A person wishing to open a current account with him would transfer a deposit to the account of the Chief Treasury at either the National Giro or at the Llandudno branch of Richard Williams's bankers, Williams Deacon's, both of which he stressed were his bankers and not his clearing agents. (Williams Deacon's Bank merged with Glyn Mills, to become Williams-Glyn's in 1971, later absorbing the small Ireland-originated National Bank, and merging with the Royal Bank of Scotland in 1985. The present Royal Bank of Scotland premises in Llandudno are a 1973 rebuild of the former Williams Deacon's used by Williams.)

His bills of exchange regime made all the difference between his enterprise being classified as a bank – institutions subject to onerous Government restrictions – or a fascinating freelance treasury, wading through the quagmire of banking law. Customers wishing to draw against their deposit would complete a payment order in much the same manner as they would make out a cheque. A third party receiving one of these orders would pay it into his own bank or Giro account. It would then be sent to the bankers of the Chief Treasury of Wales from where it would be returned to Mr. Williams for approval. At that stage the bank would debit the account of the Chief Treasury of Wales while the Chief Treasury, in their books, would debit the account of the customer. Despite the complexity of the system the Chief Treasury of Wales claimed their commission charges were lower than those of the clearing banks. The novelty of the system was that Richard Williams launched a bank in everything but name, with 35,000 ready-made branches, i.e. 23,000 Post Office Giro counters and 12,000 clearing banks. The system worked smoothly, with his payment orders being accepted by third parties as far afield as London and Aldershot and then passing through the country's cheque-clearing network.

At each stage Williams, an active lecturing Associate of the Institute of Bankers, merely wished to demonstrate a point and establish a precedent. His machinations were of little interest outside the specialised world of finance – or so he thought! In fact the registered title of Prif Trysorfa Cymru Limited was causing great embarrassment in Government circles, once the meaning became known to non-Welsh speakers in London. On 24 February 1969, the Board of Trade wrote to him at some length, and quoted extracts from a comprehensive dossier they had compiled relating to his activities. "*On 12th October 1968,*" they pleaded, "*you wrote to the Registrar of Companies enclosing the documents to lead to the registration of the above-named company and stating that* 'The best translation of the company name, which is of course in Welsh, coming as it does from a Welsh seaside town, is The Chief Treasurehouse of Wales.' *The Registrar had no reason to doubt your statement and accordingly did not check the accuracy of that translation.*"

On 1 November 1998, continued the Board of Trade letter, Williams wrote to them saying "any future registration of a company entitled Bank of Wales Ltd. would be too similar to be acceptable without causing our company trading embarrassment."

"On 21 November 1968 you wrote to the Prime Minister's Secretary enclosing a copy of a letter you had written on the same date to certain banks about Computer Consultants Limited's dispute with them. That letter contains the following: *'Obviously it is desirable for all the banks to agree to enter into such arrangements with us. The only organisation at present authorised by us to make use of these encoding techniques is Prif Trysorfa Cymru Ltd (Chief Treasury of Wales Ltd) which recently came into being and which is popularly described as the 'Bank of Wales'.*"

Eventually returning to the point of their initial mistranslation of the company's name, the letter continued: "*I am informed that Prif Trysorfa Cymru unquestionably means Chief Treasury of Wales, and that 'treasurehouse' would in Welsh be 'trysordy', not 'trysorfa'. In the circumstances the Board have to consider whether they ought to exercise the power conferred on them by section 46 (1) of the Companies Act, 1967, to direct the company to change its name. The name Chief Treasury of Wales suggests a financial institution having greater resources than a share capital of £100. Moreover it suggests an institution enjoying some form of Government or other official status or sponsorship.*"

The letter concluded by inviting Williams to answer three questions: (1) the precise nature of his company's activities; (2) how much of an article about him in *The Economist* of 11 January 1969 did he accept and how much (if any) he would dispute; and (3) what alternative name could he suggest for the company. *The Economist* feature troubling the Government was headed "Welsh Banking Cuckoo", and it posed the question: "*How do you launch a new commercial bank with 35,000 ready-made branches throughout Britain; not a single one of them your own?*" The article then set out the way in which the Chief Treasury of Wales operated its "payment orders", stating it was a bank for all practical purposes. "*But it has still to be proved that an appeal to Welsh nationalism plus admiration for gallant entrepreneurial originality can overcome some fundamental disadvantages,*" added the article.

To this Williams replied, on 4 March 1969: "Your letter does not seem to me to have been written with the purpose of helping us with our activities." He said no responsibility rested upon him or his company to translate Welsh phrases for the Civil Service. He pointed out that London civil servants would have access to the *Collins-Spurrell Welsh Dictionary*, in which "trysorfa" was rendered into English as "treasury". He also quoted the *Readers' Digest Great Encyclopaedia Dictionary* in which *"treasury"* was described as *"a room or building in which precious or valuable objects are preserved"*. As with so many translations from one language to another it was largely a matter of taking your pick in trying to decide the precise meaning of a word. "It would be very wrong just to guess that an important company which was in the course of being registered might only be a curio shop at the end of a seaside town pier," he wrote.

Having been invited to describe the company's activities Williams added: *"(we) are in the process of preparing to issue Welsh Treasury Notes which will have, as their backing, English currency, and which are, of course, merely promissory notes payable on demand, properly issued in Welsh by a British registered limited liability company. Our plans are ambitious and we are currently in correspondence with a number of foreign people with the expectation of being able to arrange a fixed rate of exchange for our Welsh Treasury Notes in terms of foreign currency."*

Spelling out the significance of his intentions, Williams said: *"We are not fundamentally interested in the local butcher, baker or candlestick maker using these Welsh Treasury Notes, but there is a great interest in using them as a means of exchanging foreign currency, including English pounds, for foreign currency to facilitate trade without unnecessary restrictions from international exchange control formalities ... Such facilities will, undoubtedly, assist in making Wales more important from an international finance point of view, and consequently more economically viable."* He added that this was encompassed by his declared intentions, within the company's memorandum of association, "to promote all interests in Wales", and as 1969 was a year to be devoted to celebrating the Investiture of Prince Charles, as Prince of Wales, at Caernarfon Castle, it seemed an ideal time to promote his scheme.

"I hope that in these activities we can count upon the co-operation of everyone, and that you will not send us any further letters which, however well-intentioned, give us the distinct impression of being unhelpful and unconstructive," he concluded, at the same time warning the Board of Trade he would seek substantial financial compensation if forced to change the company's name.

True to his threat to issue Welsh Treasury Notes, Williams used bilingual company letter headings and a typewriter to make four Welsh promissory notes for 10 shillings, £1, £5 and £10, which he sent to the Somerset House tax stamping office of the Board of Inland Revenue, on 10 March 1969. The letter heading gave the name *"Prif Trysorfa Cymru Cyfyngedig (Chief Treasury of Wales Limited)"* but otherwise the wording was entirely in Welsh: *"Y mae Prif Trysorfa Cymru Ltd yn gaddo talu y perchenog y swm o* (with appropriate value) *pan yr hawlio."* Welsh orthographers might have tidied up the grammar, but the meaning was clear enough: The Chief Treasury of Wales was promising to pay the owner on demand. The notes were signed by R. Hugh Williams and Eirlys E. Williams. After some days delay, while Inland Revenue staff no doubt consulted a few legal and Welsh

PRIF TRYSORFA CYMRU CYFYNGEDIG

(CHIEF TREASURY OF WALES LIMITED)

7604

Y mae Prif Trysorfa Cymru Limited yn

gaddo talu y perchenog y swm o

UN PUNT

£1

pan yr hawlio.

Dros Prif Trysorfa Cymru Limited

£1

Eilys E Williams
Cyfarwyddwr. 10/3/69.

G.P.O. Box 8, Llandudno, Wales.

604

language advisers in London and Cardiff, the four notes were given the impressive blue impressed stamp of Somerset House, bearing the Royal crown (whose style they had forgotten to change from that used for the reign of King George VI, before the accession of Queen Elizabeth II in 1952). Stamp duty of one penny was introduced in 1853 as a standard replacement for the former *ad valorum* tax, which had varied according to the value of the note. The stamp duty was increased to two pence in 1918, and was embossed on every promissory note and cheque.

A precedent had been established and the way was open for Williams to start printing his money.

In a subliminal expression of pan-Celtic solidarity, it was on St. Patrick's Day 1969 that the world first heard of Richard Williams's Welsh pound notes, attractively designed and all neatly embossed with the two-penny tax stamp of the Liverpool office of the Board of Inland Revenue, the date 17-3-69 minutely woven into the design incorporating the Crown and the national floral symbols of rose, thistle, daffodil, shamrock and oak leaves.

Inspired by the attention then being concentrated on preparations for the Investiture of the Prince of Wales, the back of the note carried a delightful full-colour representation of Caernarfon Castle and quayside. It was reproduced from a watercolour by a forgotten artist named A.Netherwood. Little was known about the artist, apart from the fact that he (or she) appended RCA to the signature, indicating that he/she was a member of the Royal Cambrian Academy, at Plas Mawr, Conwy, where the artist was thought to have Shropshire connections. There was a woman artist of the same name who used to work from a studio in Marl Lane, Deganwy, during the 1920s and 1930s. The original picture was to be found on one of the walls of Williams's home, at 19 Roumania Drive, Llandudno, where he had considerable sentimental attachment to it, having known it on one of the walls of his childhood home at Caernarfon. The notes were printed by Craig-y-don Printers, Llandudno.

There were slight changes from the wording on the typewritten prototypes stamped at Somerset House a week earlier (and still lacking grammatical perfection). Apart from the word "Limited", as required by company law, no English was used on the front, which read: *Y mae Prif Trysorfa Cymru Limited yn gaddo talu a cludwr pan yr hawlio y swm o Un Punt*. This translated as: "The Chief Treasury of Wales Ltd. promises to pay the bearer on demand the sum of one pound." They were signed individually "R.Hugh Williams". An English explanation, rather than a translation, was superimposed on the picture on the reverse: *"This promissory note drawn by the Chief Treasury of Wales Limited promises to pay the bearer on demand the sum of one pound sterling."* The notes were also decorated with the abacus symbol of his Computer Consultants Ltd.

On 19 March Williams put up two notices, one in the window of a somewhat insignificant former Co-op grocery shop in Peniel Street, Deganwy, and the other on the door of a bedroom at the Cora Hotel, in Upper Woburn Place, London WC1. They stated: *"Welsh Treasury Notes issued and exchanged here. Hours of business: 1.30-2.30 pm,"* and Williams invited the Press to meet him at his new Chief Treasury of Wales to watch history being made. A group of curious people gathered outside the Deganwy Treasury – watched by a policeman charged with the task of ascertaining whether something illegal was going on.

Deg Swllt

This Promisory Note drawn by the Chief Treasury of Wales Limited promises to pay the bearer on demand the sum of ten shillings sterling.

Collectors fortunate enough to possess one of that first batch of pioneering Welsh pound notes will be pleased to know how few were stamped on 17 March. There were only forty-nine £1 notes, despite the six-figure serial numbering used to create the impression there were at least 100,000 in circulation. In addition there were one hundred with a face value of ten shillings, and twenty-six each, valued at £5 and £10. The quantities were small because they were never intended to be more than a token issue, to prove a point and establish what Williams believed would be his copyright in the mysterious black patch incorporated in the design. It will be remembered that Williams had failed to patent his machine-readable numeric cheque encoding system which, after being taken up and developed by American banks, came to be known as E-13B – which was no more than an identification for the particular type font. It was quickly taken up by all the British banks which, since October 1968, had been receiving copyright royalty invoices from Williams.

By that time Williams had written and published several books on electronic banking and had decided that the E-13B system should be replaced by something infinitely superior and more secure, in the form of computer readable magnetic data, hidden from unauthorised eyes behind a dark patch – what we now have on the backs of our bank credit cards. It was with the intention of establishing what he thought would be a copyright in this development that he issued his St. Patrick's Day Welsh promissory notes, knowing the Press would devour the story of the little man printing his own money with Government approval. That would enable him to establish both the publicity and irrefutable international dating for the start of his perceived "copyright". Many of those pioneering notes, especially the £1 value, were bought by transient journalists, to be discarded as that day's waste paper once the story was written.

Unwittingly, however, Williams had captured the imagination of collectors across the globe who store thousands of bank notes in albums, and of whose existence he was unaware. Within hours of the newspaper stories he was flooded with enquiries from people wanting to buy his money – with no intention of ever redeeming the notes. He was sitting on a potential fortune, but had not printed enough Welsh money to feed the market. By way of adding authentication and collectors' value to his money, and much to his surprise, a man turned up at his Llandudno home on 20 August 1969, saying he was from Lloyds Bank's long-forgotten "Walks Department". He presented one of Williams's original £1 notes, No. 100136, bearing the crossing: *Lloyds Bank Ltd., Holborn Circus, London EC1*. It was the first of his Welsh pound notes to be redeemed, having passed through the bank clearing system.

There was an even stranger visit to Williams's home on 4 December. Llandudno Police Station first telephoned him and asked: "Is that the Chief Treasury of Wales?" A voice went on to say a woman had used one of Williams's £5 notes to pay an assistant for goods bought at a shop in Ruthin. The shopkeeper had taken the note to Ruthin Police Station, believing himself to be the victim of a confidence trick. The note had been sent on to Llandudno as a suspected fraud. "You redeem the note by walking along to 19 Roumania Drive – I'll be here for the next hour," replied Richard Williams. The author was present when, a few minutes later, Police Constable 82 William Jones cycled up to the house and presented the note, for which he was given five Bank of England £1 notes. "Is that all, isn't there anything to sign?" asked the baffled policeman. Perhaps this was the first and only time in history for the police to act as banker's agents.

Meanwhile, beyond the orbit of police suspicion, Williams's Welsh money assumed instant political significance among a people who had been so vividly reminded that they were the only citizens of the British Commonwealth without their own currency. Scotland had been printing its own money since 1696, and in 1969 still had three note-issuing banks: the Bank of Scotland, Clydesdale Bank and Royal Bank of Scotland. Northern Ireland had been issuing its own money since 1922, and in 1969 enjoyed the notes of four banks: the Bank of Ireland (Belfast), Northern Bank, Provincial Bank of Ireland (Belfast) and Ulster Bank. Even the Isle of Man, Jersey and Guernsey had their own notes. England had the prestige of the Bank of England but its last independent bank notes were withdrawn in 1921, when Fox, Fowler & Co., of Wellington, Somerset, merged with Lloyds. Wales has been without indigenous bank notes since the 1908 withdrawal of the North & South Wales Bank issue (following its merger with Midland Bank), and even those were not in the Welsh language. The first banking concession to the Welsh language was in 1965 when Midland Bank introduced bilingual cheques at their Welsh branches. The same wording, *taler* (pay) and *neu a enwo* (or order), was adopted soon after by the National Provincial Bank, and later still by all the banks at their Welsh branches.

Williams believed he had created the first Welsh-language pound note, and indeed so he had in his native Wales. However one of the first acts of the 153 pioneers who set up the Welsh colony in Patagonia, Argentina, in 1865, was to print their own £1 and 10-shilling notes. The world's first Welsh pound note was inscribed *Mae Gwladychfa Gymreig Patagonia yn cydnabod y Nodyn hwn am un*

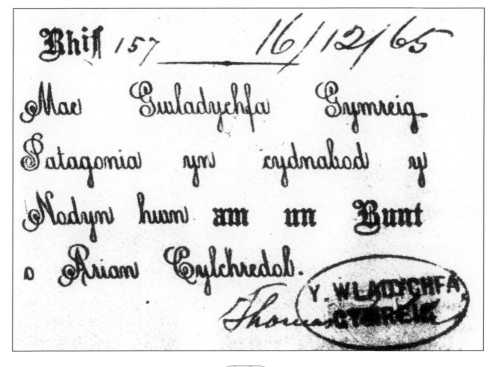

Bunt o Arian Cylchredol. Not exactly the wording of a promissory note as required under English law, the inscription translates as: "The Patagonia Welsh Settlement acknowledges this note for One Pound of regional money." There was a matching inscription on the 10s notes. The settlers arrived at the mouth of the Chubut Valley on 28 July, and by 9 August they were trading with their own Welsh paper money, using the sterling denominations of the land they had abandoned. The early notes were signed by the colony's co-founder Lewis Jones, who, like Richard Williams of a century later, hailed from Caernarfon. Lewis Jones's daughter Eluned Morgan was to have a long romance with William George, brother of politician David Lloyd George. The George brothers later became involved in a shady Patagonian gold exploration venture which, if successful, might have given some credibility to a Welsh "regional money". The Welsh colony survives, but now uses the *pesos* of the Argentine Republic – where the head office of the Argentine National Bank, at Buenos Aires, is roofed with Welsh slates from Llechwedd Slate Mines, at Blaenau Ffestiniog.

Having discovered the collectors' market for his notes Williams promptly arranged for a reprint, next day, of all four denominations, which his wife took by train to the Manchester Stamp Office. She had to return to Llandudno without them, and on 21 March Williams received a letter, bearing the previous day's date, from the Secretary (Taxes) at Somerset House, stating: "*I am directed by the Board of Inland Revenue to refer to two thousand documents you have sent to Manchester Stamp Office, for stamping. I am to say that Section 7, of The Bank Notes Act, 1826, prevents the Inland Revenue from stamping any promissory note or the form of any promissory note for the payment to the bearer on demand of any sum of money less than £5, and as the Board are advised that the documents referred to come within the description the Stamp Office is unable to stamp them and they will be returned to you.*"

With the letter was a photocopy of the 1826 Act which stipulated a fixed penalty of £20 for every promissory note made, signed, issued, or re-issued in contravention of Section 7, adding: "*The commissioners shall not be empowered to provide any stamp or stamps for expressing or denoting the duty or duties payable in England upon any promissory note for the payment to the bearer on demand of any sum of money less than the sum of five pounds; nor shall it be lawful for the said commissioners, or any of their officers, to stamp any promissory note or the form of any promissory note, for the payment to the bearer on demand of any sum of money less than five pounds.*"

Although the clause made reference only to England, the Tax Secretary hastened to advise Mr. Williams that the Wales & Berwick Act, 1747, ruled that all statutory references to England embraced the Dominion of Wales. That legislation came about because of 18th century doubts about the liability of the residents of Berwick-upon-Tweed to pay window tax. The Welsh Language Act, 1967, repealed the clause about the Dominion of Wales – but only for post-1967 legislation.

"The Board have been informed that some 200 similar documents were presented to the Liverpool Stamp Office on Monday, 17th, and that these were stamped. Such of those notes as were for sums of less than £5 should not have been stamped and I am to express the Board's regret for this error," added the Tax Secretary.

Williams took that to be a full confession that Inland Revenue were as guilty as himself in their common contravention of the 1826 Act, and would not be asking him to pay the £42,980 penalty to which he had exposed himself. He, however, was not so contrite. He replied to the Tax Secretary, pointing out that Somerset House had initiated the error by stamping the four typewritten prototype notes for 10s, £1, £5 and £10 on 10 March. They had also stamped his batch of notes on 17

March. With their having twice endorsed his notes he had proceeded to print a very large quantity, of which the 2,000 sent for stamping on 21 March were only a small proportion. *"We therefore reserve our position in respect of loss and damages against the Board of Inland Revenue and individual officials whose names we will, if necessary, demand,"* he added.

When Williams spoke to Somerset House by telephone, to clarify their intentions about the £5 and £10 notes still at Manchester, Inland Revenue said they would be stamped that day. They also offered to reimburse the 2d duty they had illegally charged on any 10s and £1 notes he cared to surrender to them for cancellation. That, of course, immediately inflated the value of the Government-endorsed illegal notes and within a day or two they were changing hands for £50.

With his flair for highlighting the absurd, Williams convened a Press conference to announce it had always been his desire to comply with the law while printing his own money, and having had his attention drawn to the 1747 and 1826 legislation, requiring him to confine himself to note issues for more than £5, he had commenced to issue notes for £100,000. In fact only one such note was printed, again by Craig-y-don Printers, and received the Government's 2d tax endorsement at the Manchester Stamp Office on 24 March.

Things were by then moving rapidly in the London Establishment. On 26 March the Board of Trade served Williams with a formal note saying: *"Whereas the Board of Trade are of the opinion that the name by which Prif Trysorfa Cymru Limited is registered gives so misleading an indication of the nature of its activities as to be likely to cause harm to the public; the Board, in exercise of the power conferred on them by Section 46 of the Companies Act, 1967, hereby direct Prif Trysorfa Cymru Limited to change its name within a period of six weeks from the date hereof."*

Williams's initial reaction was to contest the directive – the first of its kind under the 1967 Act – for he believed a patriotic Welsh court would lend him a sympathetic ear. Collectors saw the Government departments ganging up against the Welsh entrepreneur and his home-made money, and they rushed to buy up the remaining £5 and £10 notes of the short-lived Chief Treasury of Wales. To meet their desire to own his 10s and £1 notes Williams overprinted the 2,000 that had been returned unstamped on 21 March, with the words "Cancelled by Order", and sold them to the souvenir trade, where they retailed at 5s each, for either denomination. However, they were on the market for less than a week, being withdrawn as soon as Williams devised yet another tweak of the snarling London Government's tail.

Poring over his banking law books, Williams decided that if the Board of Trade was prepared to quote 1747 legislation to him, he could go one better and make use of the 1724 introduction of "bank post bills". These were devised as a means of transmitting money by post while keeping it safe from highway robbers. The bills were payable at three, and later seven days "after sight", and 60-day bills were introduced in 1836. Bank post bills existed until 1934.

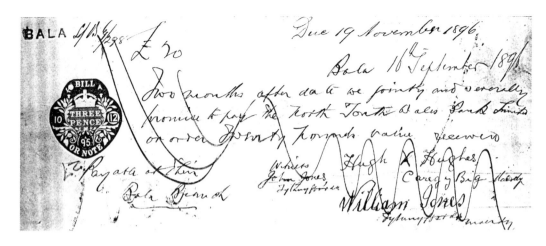

Once again Williams went back to his printer with a very slightly amended design for a new run of 10s and £1 notes bearing the name of the Chief Treasury of Wales, which was living out its last six weeks. The legend read: *"Y mae Prif Trysorfa Cymru Limited yn gaddo talu a cludwr un diwrnod ar ol ei golwg a swm o Un Punt."* The new English explanation (rather than a direct translation) on the back of the note, said: *"This Promissory Note drawn by the Chief Treasury of Wales Limited promises to pay the bearer one day after sight the sum of one pound sterling."*

Also incorporated in the design of the sight bills were two black sheep – a hidden message of more Welsh trouble being brewed for the beleaguered Boards of Trade and Inland Revenue in their London fortresses. By that time the author, in his role of political correspondent for the *Daily Post,* was seeing Williams almost daily, and, upon learning that the name of Chief Treasury of Wales had been outlawed, he suggested that as Williams was clearly seen as the black sheep of the world of finance he should revive the romantic 19th century name by which the Aberystwyth & Tregaron Bank was usually known, because of the design of its notes: Banc y Ddafad Ddu, meaning Black Sheep Bank.

Williams sent a specimen of each new note to Somerset House on 29 March, with a cheque for the 4d total tax. On 1 April he was told the Inland Revenue solicitors were studying his notes – perhaps believing they were an April Fool's Day joke. On 5 April he demanded a decision, and on 8 April the notes were stamped and returned to him. He quickly delivered a packet of 10s and £1 notes to the Manchester Stamp Office, where they received the tax stamp on 17 April, just one month after the start of this remarkably newsy saga. He had obtained 1,500 of each value but only a few were stamped before he ran out of time. The surplus was overprinted "Cancelled by Order" and sold to the collectors' market.

Williams's last act before obeying the order to change his Treasury's name was to print a single note for £1,000,000. He successfully argued that it was for a sum in excess of £5, as required by the 1826 Act, and it was duly endorsed with the Government's tax stamp at Somerset House.

Y mae **PRIF TRYSORFA CYMRU LIMITED**
yn gaddo talu y cludwr un diwrnod ar ol ei golwg
y swm o   *Un Punt*
N° 103201
                              LLANDUDNO.

                    Dros Prif Trysorfa Cymru Limited

1
Punt

1
Punt

TWO PENCE

Cyfarwyddwr.

N° 103201

Y mae **PRIF TRYSORFA CYMRU LIMITED**
yn gaddo talu y cludwr un diwrnod ar ol ei golwg
y swm o   *Deg Swllt*
N° 12701
                              LLANDUDNO.

                    Dros Prif Trysorfa Cymru Limited

10
Swllt

10
Swllt

TWO PENCE

Cyfarwyddwr.

N° 12701

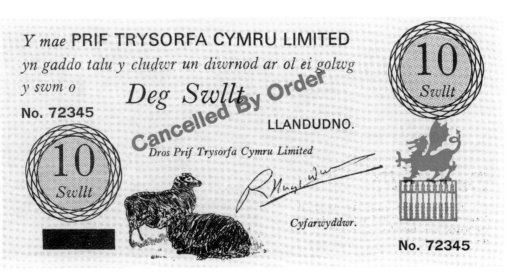

Y mae **PRIF TRYSORFA CYMRU LIMITED**
yn gaddo talu y cludwr un diwrnod ar ol ei golwg
y swm o   *Deg Swllt*
No. 72345
                              LLANDUDNO.

                    Dros Prif Trysorfa Cymru Limited

10
Swllt

10
Swllt

Cyfarwyddwr.

No. 72345

Somewhere in the London corridors of power the day got off to a bad start for some hapless Government servant when he opened a letter from that troublesome Welshman Richard Williams, notoriously printing his own money. This time the problem was the rebel's abject desire to comply with the order to change the name of his company, for which he proposed the alternative title of Cwmni y Ddafad Ddu Gymreig Ltd. But what on earth did it mean? Having made an embarrassing mess of translating the first name, the Board of Trade consulted the Welsh Office, in nearby Parliament Street. In due course it was established that there were no hidden catches in the new name. Williams wanted to exchange his grandiose Establishment-quaking Chief Welsh Treasury for the unbelievably humble self-effacing and almost apologetic "Welsh Black Sheep Company". The change was duly approved with a certificate dated 30 April 1969.

The last laugh was, of course, with Richard Williams. When used in Wales the name of Cwmni y Ddafad Ddu meant something entirely different from its simple translation into English. Before today's dilution of Welsh history by shallow televised globalisation, and the mortification of the intellect by loud tuneless rhythmic monotony, generations of children had been told the story of the romantic bank notes of Banc y Ddafad Ddu, meaning the Black Sheep Bank. This was the popular name for the Aberystwyth & Tregaron Bank, opened in about 1810, at Bridge Street, Aberystwyth, by John Evans, Joseph Jones and William Davies. The unofficial name was derived from the bank's incorporation of one black ewe on its £1 note, with two sheep on the £2 note, for easy identification by the illiterate (at a time when few people could read).

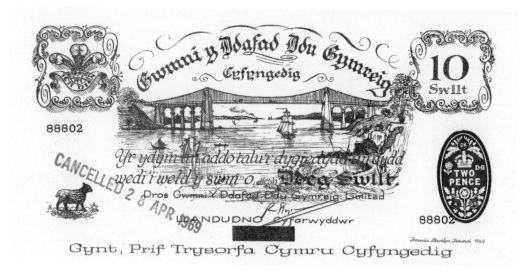

A new note for Williams's Black Sheep "bank" had already been designed by the author –sketched out on Williams's desk, at his Llandudno home, and then given to local commercial artist Francis Llewelyn Traversi for drawing. It was based upon the last note issue of the North & South Wales Bank, using Thomas Telford's Menai suspension bridge of 1826 as the main feature. As his model for this issue Mr.Traversi was given an 1830 steel engraving (by J.W.Ambrose, of Bangor) from the author's collection. Features such as the Prince of Wales's feathers and the frame denoting the value were retained from the North & South Wales Bank design, but sheep were added from the Aberystwyth & Tregaron Bank precedent. In similar fashion to the North & South Wales Bank issue, the company's name was arched over the bridge as Cwmni y Ddafad Ddu Gymreig Cyfyngedig, i.e. entirely in Welsh, by translating the "Limited" of the registered title.

Basically the same as on his first "one day after sight" test issue, the wording had been tidied up by Ffowc Williams, a member of the Gorsedd of Bards of Wales, and a neighbour of the man who by then had been dubbed "Williams the Money" by several newspapers. This time the promise read: *"Yr ydym yn addo talu'r dygiedydd un dydd wedi'i weld y swm o Un Bunt."* There was matching wording for the 10s notes, and the slightly different "on demand" promise on the £5 and £10 notes: *"Yr ydym yn addo talu'r dygiedydd pan yr hawlio y swm o ... (amount)."* They were signed by Richard Williams *"Dros Cwmni y Ddafad Ddu Gymreig Ltd.",* (i.e. "on behalf of the Welsh Black Sheep Co. Ltd").

If the Government thought they had seen the last of the Chief Treasury's money they were much mistaken, for in large print, across the bottom of the new Black Sheep notes were the words: *"Gynt, Prif Trysorfa Cymru Cyfyngedig",* meaning "Formerly the Chief Treasury of Wales Ltd." Following the system of symbols used by the original Black Sheep Bank, in 19th century Aberystwyth, Williams decorated his notes with a ewe for £1 and introduced a lamb for 10s. To avoid cluttering his notes with a flock of sheep he used a ram for £5 and two rams for £10. Williams said the symbols would facilitate reading by the 81% of non-Welsh speaking citizens of Wales.

Forty of these notes were produced bearing the authenticity of the Government's embossed 2d tax stamp, dated 28 April 1969, but blank on the reverse. There were twelve for 10s, ten for £1, ten for £5 and eight for £10. They were rubberstamped "cancelled" on the front and were especially prepared for distribution to newspapers in time for the announcement about the change of company name two days later.

The first notes issued after the change became effective incorporated, as a reverse design, the full colour painting of Caernarfon Castle that had appeared on all the notes of the Chief Treasury of Wales, thus maintaining a subliminal link in the public mind. The innovative English wording superimposed on the painting on the reverse contained a hidden threat, which the Government failed to recognise for three months. It said: *"This Promissory Note drawn by the Black Sheep Company of Wales Limited formerly the Chief Treasury of Wales Limited promises to pay the bearer one day after sight the sum of not less than One Pound sterling."* Twenty of each denomination were taxed on 6 May 1969.

At that time United Kingdom residents were restricted as to the amount of sterling they could take abroad at any one time and in any one year. In promising to pay "not less than One Pound sterling" Williams was giving notice that his Welsh pound notes, issued at Llandudno, might be worth more than the Bank of England variety! *"There is nothing to prevent Cwmni y Ddafad Ddu Gymreig Ltd giving permission for their notes to be printed in Germany, Switzerland and the United States of America, and issued against an agreed deposit in a bank of each country,"* he told the author, adding: *"It follows that if the value of the pound sterling fell in relation to the currencies of these countries the Welsh pound would be worth more than the English pound."*

To test the status of his Welsh money in relation to the controlled amount of sterling one could export, Mr. Williams took a flight to Yugoslavia on 16 April 1969. The Exchange Control Act, 1947, forbade British citizens from taking abroad more than £50 a year in sterling or its foreign equivalent, all the transactions being entered in one's passport. Additionally one could take out £15 that had to be shown on return to Britain, in whole or by way of receipts for sums spent on returning British-owned aircraft or ships. This £15 was intended to facilitate one's journey home after entering British territory. (The same draconian Act also forbade the retention of gold coins minted after 1837, a prohibition which lucky holders of sovereigns secretly ignored.)

At Heathrow airport Mr. Williams declared to H.M.Customs that in addition to his holiday allocation of pounds and *dinars* he was carrying £15 in Chief Welsh Treasury notes, which he produced, and at the same time asked for a ruling. There was considerable confusion, with a parade of Customs officers in an ascending pecking order of seniority coming to look at his Welsh money, and then disappearing for some hidden consultation. Unable to find anything in their rulebook that offered any guidance for such a crisis, they eventually arrived at a compromise: Williams could retain his homemade £15 provided he gave a solemn promise to bring the notes back from Yugoslavia. Upon his return to Heathrow Williams was asked to produce his Welsh money, which he did, at the same time giving notice that on his next trip he would be carrying his £100,000 Welsh Treasury note, by which time he would expect H.M.Customs to be able to quote a legal ruling on his money.

News of his Celtic stand prompted a Scottish businessman to place £15 in Scottish notes in his wallet, in addition to his £50 allowance, when flying out of Glasgow airport. He wanted to argue his case to H.M.Customs that Scottish

currency was outside the Exchange Control Act, because it was not legal tender, but unfortunately he was let through without any check. When he got to Italy the Banco di Roma readily exchanged his Scottish pounds for Italian *lira,* thus giving him an extra £15 of spending money in the belief he had not broken English law.

The story might have ended there but in June the anomalous status of Celtic money was highlighted in the House of Commons, when James Davison, MP for Aberdeen West, asked whether Bank of England or Scottish bank notes remained legal tender after being permanently stained by a device that operated in the event of theft. Treasury Minister of State Dick Taverne replied: *"Such staining should not affect the legal status of Bank of England notes. Scottish banknotes are not legal tender."*

With shades of Richard Williams, lawyer Winifred Ewing, Scottish Nationalist MP for Hamilton, suggested there was nothing to stop a Scottish citizen taking caseloads of his non-legal tender Scottish money out of the United Kingdom. *"It should be impossible for the Government to say on the one hand that Scottish notes are not legal, and on the other refuse permission to take them out of the country. I doubt whether H.M.Customs would have the nerve to prosecute a Scot for taking his banknotes abroad when the Government says they are not legal tender,"* said Mrs. Ewing, adding that the question needed to be made the subject of a test case in the courts.

In a delayed response the Treasury said: *"Although there has never been a test case on this issue, as far as we know, our advice is that it is covered by Section 22, of the Exchange Control Act, which refers to the control or export of sterling notes of a class which is, or has been, legal tender in the United Kingdom. As far as practice goes, it is our understanding that Customs officers count Scottish notes in."*

Clutching at straws, the "has been" phrase was seized upon by the Treasury because for a brief period, during World War Two, Scottish notes were given the status of legal tender, for "the duration of the present emergency", as a precaution against the breakdown of communications with London in the event of an enemy invasion.

"Sheer Government gobbledegook! What on earth are they trying to say about either Scottish or Welsh money," retorted Richard Williams – and another ten years were to elapse before the Government abolished exchange control (resulting in the 1979 closure of an enormous department of the Bank of England).

On 7 June Richard Williams unexpectedly received a certificate from the Celtic Brotherhood, in Park Lane, New York, informing him he had been elected a member, with the bardic title of *Williams the Money*, in recognition of his pioneering work in the interests of Wales. With the certificate was a letter beginning: *"Dear Richard, We've sent your money to the highest in the banking world, USA. Your money has a wonderful attractive design. Well done Richard."*

The Celtic Brotherhood told him he had become one of the world's ten million members of the International Chieftain Commandos, whose other affiliated sister organisations comprised: Patriotic Friends of Zion, Mizo Nationalists, American Devolutionists, Naga Christian Nationalists, Ukrainian Nationalists, Lithuanian Freedom Army, Estonian Patriots, Tibetan Nationalists, Patriots of Manchu, Basque Independence Organisations, Breton Nationalists, United Irelanders, Greenland Freedom Association, Quebec Independence Society, Ancient Brother-hood of Irish Chieftains, Fellowship of St. Patrick, Nationalist Press Officers Association, Celtic Patriotic League of America, Canadian Irish Association, Bahama Internal Independence Group and the Canton Nationalists.

Following substantial orders for his notes from two American dealers (S.R.Williams, in Cassopolis, Michigan, and Gary F.Snover, of San Bernardino, California), Richard Williams opened an account in the name of Cwmni y Ddafad Ddu Gymreig at the First Commercial Savings Bank of Cassopolis, and announced to the world that his former Chief Treasury of Wales now had six note-issuing branches in the United States. Cassopolis was a remote town of only 2,027 inhabitants, but its busy little bank boasted of branches at Constantine (population 1,710), Union City (1,669), White Pigeon (1,399), Edwardsburg (902) and Diamond Lake.

Initially the First Commercial Savings Bank of Cassopolis had to overcome an 1863 Act, adopted during the American Civil War, declaring the issue of all private bank notes illegal in the United States. The Act was passed at a time of considerable confusion, when there were several thousand banks of issue across America. In 1852 Rhode Island had a bank of issue for every 2,000 inhabitants, whereas Pennsylvania, which by 1850 was already an industrial and commercial centre, with a big Welsh population, had only one bank of issue for every 40,000 of its citizens. Transport facilities were all-important in the vastness of America. In theory a traveller should be able to convert his notes anywhere, but in practice people were wary of accepting notes other than those issued by a bank with which they were familiar. How familiar, asked the Cassopolis bankers, would be the people of White Pigeon, Michigan, with a note of the Black Sheep Bank issued at Llandudno? Williams soon persuaded them he was not a private banker but the Welsh Chief Treasurer, whose promissory notes had been endorsed and embossed with nothing less than the Royal Crown of the United Kingdom, in the British Government's 2d tax stamp of approval. And so it passed that in July 1969 LeRoy G.Cox, vice-president of the First Commercial Savings Bank of Cassopolis, wrote to Williams Deacon's Bank, at Llandudno, stating that the opening of the Welsh Black Sheep account had been approved, by resolution.

Williams's money became a star feature at the coin and note collectors' convention at Los Angeles in June. Reinforcing his threat to issue his Black Sheep money abroad, on 5 September 1969 Williams registered Cwmni y Ddafad Ddu Gymreig Incorporated, at Washington DC, USA. The author was at Williams's house when a cable arrived from David A.Scott, of the legal firm Carr, Bonner, O'Connell, Kaplan & Scott, of 1001 Connecticut Avenue NW, Washington, informing him the American branch of the Llandudno enterprise had been incorporated, with the declared aims of promoting Welsh interests and issuing printed bills of exchange. Mr. Scott and two of his partners held 60% of the shares, and the remaining 40% were at the disposal of Mr. Williams, and offered to American businessman for $20 each. Among preliminary difficulties raised by the District of Columbia Superintendent of Corporations was a reference to the District of Columbia Business Corporation Act 1954, which said: "*Corporations for profit may be organised under this chapter for any lawful purpose or purposes except where the purpose is for banking or insurance.*" There was also the qualification of the older Business Corporations Law 1901, which stated: "*...excepting banks of circulation or discount, railroads, and other enterprises and business as may be specially provided for in this code.*" Mr. Scott, a member of the House of Delegates for Annapolis, Maryland, worked his way through these impediments, to create further Welsh problems for the financial institutions of London.

"*Our American sister company is only a few hours old, and the question of a takeover is only one of the many possibilities to be discussed,*" Williams told the author, adding that he was also prepared to sell his Llandudno note-issuing company to the new American company, in which event all future issues of Welsh pound notes would be made in Washington. He was asked if the United States issue of a note redeemable in either Washington or Llandudno would make nonsense of British currency control regulations – which at that time required British subjects to sell to a bank any foreign currency they acquired. "*That is a problem for the Bank of England. I wrote to the Prime Minister ten months ago informing him there was American interest in our activities,"* said Williams.

Wasting no time, he printed twenty-four £1 notes for dual British and American use, this time using his own little offset litho machine that he had installed at the old Co-op shop in Deganwy. Similar to his first Black Sheep "one day after sight" notes, they were signed by Williams as President of Cwmni y Ddafad Ddu Gymreig Incorporated, Washington & Llandudno. They were printed in black only, on white paper, with nothing on the back. They were taken to the Manchester Stamp Office that same day, and endorsed with the tax impression incorporating the date 5.9.69. There was no such stamp duty in the United States but the British Government's tax stamp impressed the Americans, and Williams was propelled into an enormous collectors' market in a land where millions of people claim Welsh ancestry.

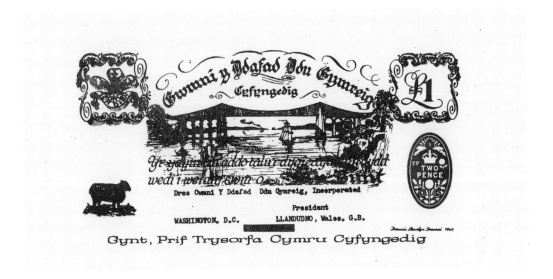

On 15 September Hywel M. Davies wrote from Piney Branch Road, Silver Spring, Maryland, telling Williams he wished to invest capital in his new Washington-based company. He said he was 31 years old, born at Loughor, Swansea, and educated at Gowerton Grammar School and Glasgow University, graduating in electrical engineering in 1961. He had worked for computer firms in Wales, Israel and the USA, and was interested in helping Cwmni y Ddafad Ddu Gymreig Inc. to develop what he described as: "a corporate shell with no officers, no capital and no definite plan".

To meet the American demand Williams produced a new note, using the original Black Sheep design, but printed in green, and payable at either Washington DC or Llandudno. *"Americans only recognise greenbacks,"* he said, but on the reverse he reproduced the painting of Caernarfon Castle used on his first Welsh treasury note. There was no translation or any other wording on the back, leaving his

Washington purchasers to ascertain the meaning of his Welsh legend. Not having settled his bill with Craig-y-don Printers, at Llandudno, for printing his pioneering notes, and unable to print in full colour on his own press, Williams was obliged to go to James Craig & Co., in Penrhyn Road, Colwyn Bay, for the printing of this run.

No tax stamp was necessary for these transatlantic notes when sold in Washington but when a collector wished to buy one at Llandudno Williams was able to comply with the tax law by attaching a 2d postage stamp. At that particular time there happened to be a special commemorative postage stamp on which the only wording was "National Giro", together with the familiar symbol for the new Giro bank, and the head of the Queen. It was valid for five-pence postage – two and a half times the tax required – but was used by Williams so as to give greater credibility, authenticity and collector value to his Welsh money. At every turn Government institutions became ensnared as unwilling co-operators in his troublesome enterprise.

When Mrs Eirlys Williams took 400 of the Welsh American notes to the Manchester Stamp Office, at Albert Bridge House, Bridge Street, on 23 June 1970, with a view to having them embossed with the 2d tax stamp, the Department wrote saying: *"It is noted that Washington DC is shown as the place of drawing. I am instructed to draw your attention to the Board of Inland Revenue's letters dated 9th January and 12th February 1970, in which it is noted that the appropriate stamp is a 2d adhesive postage stamp to be cancelled by the promisser upon its issue."* They were therefore unable to tax his notes – and thus the Government had found a way of stopping the impressive regal enhancement of his notes issued in the United States.

Formerly
The Chief Treasury of Wales Limited
Llandudno

Number

Number

Promise to pay the Bearer on demand the sum of One Hundred Welsh Pounds

£**100**

Director

Secretary

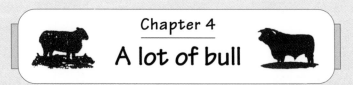

Living at Llandudno, the town enjoying the unchallengeable title of Queen of Welsh Resorts, Richard Williams's notoriety created a ready souvenir market for his money in that summer of 1969. In order to sell something cheaper than his more conventional values he decided to create a five-shilling note, for which there was at least one precedent. There was a note with the dual values of 5s and 6 francs issued by the States of Guernsey during World War One, and overprinted "British" in 1921 when the local currency was converted to sterling. There was also the quarter-guinea note issued in the mid-18th century by William Blow Collis, a mercer and draper believed to have been the founder of the earliest bank in the Midlands.

With both Williams and the author originally hailing from Caernarfon, it was not long before the conversation got around to that town's unique dialectical terms for the various units of currency. *Magan*, or *mag* was the term for a halfpenny, *niwc* for penny, *sei* for sixpence, *hog* for shilling, *hanner-bwl* for half-a-crown, *bwl* for 5s, *hanner sgrin* for 10s and *sgrin* for £1. These words will not be found in any dictionary and they have vanished from the Caernarfon vocabulary since the introduction of decimalised money. In 1969, however, *bwl* was instantly recognisable as the English "bull", a term which appeared to date back to the emergency issue of the Bank of England silver dollar, worth 5s, in 1804, followed by replacement Royal Mint crowns, which became known as bulls.

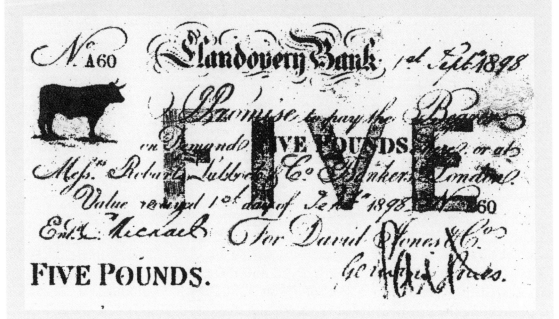

DAVID JONES
1756–1840

FOUNDER OF DAVID JONES AND CO
THE BANK OF THE BLACK OX
BANC YR EIDION DU
IN 1799

THE BANK WAS ACQUIRED BY LLOYDS BANK IN 1909
WHICH IN TURN MERGED WITH TSB IN 1999 TO BECOME
LLOYDS TSB

That, and the fame of the Llandovery Bank, better known as Banc yr Eidion Du, dictated the design for Williams's 5s notes. Banc yr Eidion Du, meaning Bank of the Black Ox, was established by David Jones at the King's Head Inn, Llanymddyfri (Llandovery), in 1799. The more familiar name was derived from Jones's incorporation of an ox on his £1 notes, symbolising the source of his trading wealth – the Welsh Black cattle which farmers of the surrounding countryside bred to provide the best roast beef of Old England. Banc yr Eidion Du became part of Lloyds Bank in 1909 but the black ox symbol survived on cheques issued at Lloyds' Llanymddyfri branch until World War Two.

Francis Traversi was asked to adapt his original Cwmni y Ddafad Ddu drawing to show a bull's head instead of the black sheep. For the back of the new Welsh notes the author supplied a World War Two five cents note issued by the Japanese Government in 1942 for use in occupied Malaya. The back of the Japanese note, printed in brown, was an intricate machine-made design depicting only the figure "5" as a readable character. As the former enemy could not claim copyright for its currency note issued during its illegal occupation of what was then a British colony, the design was freely available to Richard Williams. It was printed in green on the back of his 5s note, symbolising what he declared to be real "Welsh greenback dollars". A batch was printed and taken to Manchester, where they received the Government's tax stamp on 3 June 1969 – despite a 1775 Act prohibiting the private issue of notes for less than £1.

A week later Gwilym Williams Edwards, secretary of the Welsh Black Cattle Society, at Caernarfon, protested that the snorting bull shown on Williams's money was much too effeminate for his 1,025 members. *"It is bad for our image abroad. After a lot of hard work breeders in Wales are now exporting Welsh Black stock to places as far apart as the Falkland Islands and Uganda,"* he wrote. *"I know a bull when I see one, and I do not know what people will make of this poor creature, especially now the Welsh money is enjoying growing circulation in America, where discerning ranchers are breeding Welsh Blacks,"* said Mr. Edwards.

Something had to be done about the bull of doubtful sex, and a conference was arranged between the Welsh Black Cattle Society and the Welsh Black Sheep Company. An elated Richard Williams emerged to announce: *"We found a happy solution. New Welsh 5s notes will be issued incorporating, with permission, the official champion bull symbol of the Welsh Black Cattle Society."* To that the Society's secretary added: *"This is a modern-looking bull of which we can all be proud."* The bull was actually identifiable: it was registered as Ysbyty Ifor IIIrd, which was breed champion at the 1956 and 1957 Royal Welsh Agricultural Shows.

New notes were printed, devoid of English translation – all but about half-a-dozen bearing the Welsh word *enghraifft*, meaning "specimen" and therefore cancelling any notional exchange value. They were taxed on 18 June 1969, and the resultant publicity produced a flood of international orders for what Williams described privately, to the author, as "a load of bull". They were sold to local souvenir shops, and by the end of the month the Livestock Export Council for Wales ordered a supply of Williams's notes for distribution as souvenirs, during a six-week tour of South America, promoting Welsh Black cattle and various Welsh sheep breeds. Williams suggested they might make ideal currency for the traders in the Stock Exchange, a place where a bull was a man who bought shares with money he did not have, in the hope of making a profit by reselling before the settling day.

In August the Bank of England took exception to Williams's phrase, which he had been using since May, stating: *"...the Black Sheep Company of Wales Limited formerly the Chief Treasury of Wales Limited promises to pay the bearer one day after sight the sum of not less than One Pound sterling."* A Welsh *"punt"* meant a pound sterling, no more and no less, said the Bank. By then the citizens of Michigan (presumably bank note collectors) had deposited $2,000 in Williams's account at the First Commercial Savings Bank of Cassopolis, in exchange for his Welsh pounds, which he was selling for $2.50, being 12 cents better than the exchange rate for one of the Bank of England's pounds. *"It is the Bank's understanding that if a note issued by your company is expressed as a promise to pay a certain number of punt or swllt this means pounds or shillings,"* said the Bank of England in their letter.

"The Bank of England is demonstrably wrong for I shall continue to round up the price of my Welsh pounds to $2.50, and nobody can stop me," retorted Richard

Williams, adding: *"Their big problem is that everyone in Government is dodging the issue of defining the status of my Welsh pound. Sooner or later they must either acknowledge the existence of the Welsh punt or declare there is no such thing – in which case my money will be outside the scope of their currency control regulations, and bring about the welcome collapse of the Exchange Control Act.*

"I am considering issuing a Welsh million pound note by my Washington company, redeemable at either Washington or Llandudno. Persons acquiring such notes could transfer enormous sums back and forth across the Atlantic without the aid of banks, who are compelled to act as agents to administer our Government's currency controls," he said.

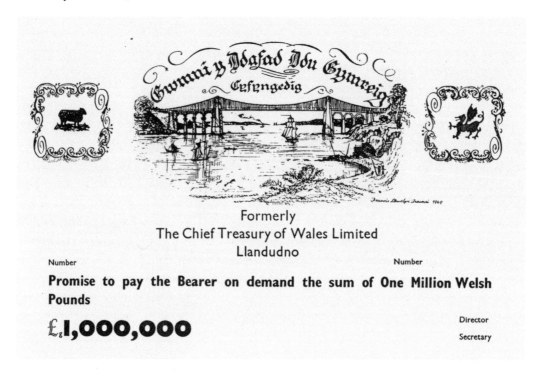

Formerly
The Chief Treasury of Wales Limited
Llandudno

Number   Number

Promise to pay the Bearer on demand the sum of One Million Welsh Pounds

£₁,000,000   Director

Secretary

Responding to pressure arising out of Richard Williams's April warning that he would be carrying a £100,000 Welsh treasury note when he next passed through Heathrow, the Bank of England advised him in September that there was no limit to the amount of these notes he took abroad, so long as none were exported to Rhodesia. British trade sanctions were then in place because of the political upheaval arising out of Ian Smith's 1965 unilateral declaration of Southern Rhodesia's independence. The Bank of England told the Press they were satisfied that the Exchange Control Act provided for all the situations that could arise from the export of home-made promissory notes. Richard Williams saw it differently, saying the mighty Bank of England was quaking in its shoes before the threat from a Welsh pound note they were trying to say did not exist.

Extracting further publicity for his money, Williams sent his million pound note, bearing the name of Prif Trysorfa Cymru, to London's New Bond Street coin specialist auctioneers Glendinings. It was unique. Two Bank of England notes for £1,000,000 were known to exist, having been produced before 1812, and used only for internal accounting processes. At the other end of the scale the Bank of England produced a bank note for one penny in 1828, again for internal accounting. Williams's note had nothing to do with accounting but was produced merely to annoy the London Establishment. Apart from the one word "Limited", required as part of the officially registered name of his company (with its limited liability to lose only £100 of shareholders' money in the event of liquidation), there was no English on his £1,000,000 note. He had relied upon the equal validity of the Welsh and English languages, stipulated by the Welsh Language Act 1967. As already noted, the Manchester Stamp Office applied its 2d tax stamp on 6 May 1969 – thereby establishing the precedent that no English translation was required on Welsh promissory notes. Williams's £1,000,000 note came up for auction on 27 November, together with an uncancelled full collection of thirty-two of his notes with a total face value of £86. Some of the notes were illustrated in the Glendining catalogue, and were listed as Lot 1. The catalogue noted: *"Wales, one of the oldest countries in Europe, is in the strange position of having no Government of its own and no money of its own. These circumstances were seized upon by Richard Williams, of Llandudno, in October 1998 when he successfully registered in Great Britain the Chief Treasury of Wales Ltd., under its Welsh title of Prif Trysorfa Cymru Ltd. In March 1969 he produced the first privately issued Welsh money, which has since caused such a financial sensation."* Bidding opened at £700 and peaked at £850 when the lot was withdrawn, not having reached the reserve price of £10,000.

Williams's next blow to the Establishment was the issue of a new set of notes illustrating various Welsh castles: Laugharne on the 10s value, Conwy on the £1 note, Harlech on the £5 and Cardiff on the £10. The design also incorporated the

Red Dragon of Wales and a single black sheep. The reverse was an adaptation of the 1942 Japanese note, to which Williams had added a dragon, a sheep, and the new words *Punt Gymraeg*. He printed them himself at his former Co-op shop, and one of the author's funniest memories is of calling there and seeing Williams ankle deep in discarded money – misprints while trying to register green, black and red ink, in separate runs, four notes to a sheet, on his rather basic litho press. The notes were taken to Manchester and taxed with the date 9 October 1969.

Announcing the birth of the *Punt Gymraeg*, meaning Welsh Pound, Williams said, on 10 October: *"The reason for the new issue is to ensure there is no question that Welsh money, which I have created at Llandudno, and which is officially recognised and impress stamped by the British Board of Inland Revenue, following very extensive research, is NOT sterling currency. Welsh pound notes are as different from English pound notes as are Egyptian or Cypriot pound notes."* (In Egypt the Arabic word for "pound" is still pronounced "ginny", clearly derived

from the English "guinea", because for most of the British occupation the exchange rate for £1 Sterling was £E1-50 milliemes.)

"*This step has been taken in view of the fact that the Bank of England, again after extensive research, make it quite clear in a letter of 15 September, that although they may be advised to the contrary they do not rule Welsh pounds to be sterling. The Bank of England also say, in a letter of 26 September, that there is no restriction on the export of Welsh pounds from the United Kingdom under the limits imposed on sterling and foreign currencies by Exchange Control regulations,*" he said.

A total of 13,000 "Welsh pound" notes were taxed before the Government discovered the meaning of *Punt Gymraeg* – or, more accurately, half discovered its meaning. In the Welsh language there are two words (plus mutations) denoting "Welsh", each with a subtle difference in meaning. *Cymraeg/Gymraeg* always relates to the Welsh language, while *Cymreig/Gymreig* means appertaining to Wales. Williams was himself confused on this point for while he had correctly used

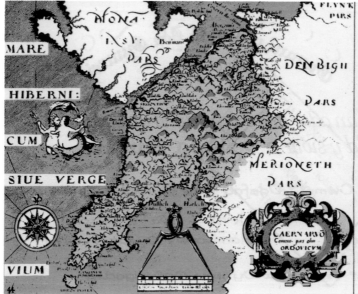

This Treasury Note promises to pay the Bearer, one day after sight, the sum of HALF A WELSH POUND

The Chief Treasury of Wales was formed in 1969 as the only privately owned National Treasury in the World and until the abolition of Stamp Duty, its Notes carried a two penny British government impressed stamp.

It later changed its name to the Black Sheep Company of Wales, some of the oldest banks in Wales being drovers banks, which later became part of the foundation of present day British Clearing Banks.

This particular note is modelled on the notes of the Aberystwyth and Tregaron Bank Ltd, that had a motif of a sheep and a lamb and was widely accepted and known as The Black Sheep Bank.

This Treasury Note promises to pay the Bearer, one day after sight, the sum of ONE WELSH POUND

The Chief Treasury of Wales was formed in 1969 as the only privately owned National Treasury in the World and until the abolition of Stamp Duty, its Notes carried a two penny British government impressed stamp.

It later changed its name to the Black Sheep Company of Wales, some of the oldest banks in Wales being drovers banks, which later became part of the foundation of present day British Clearing Banks.

This particular note is modelled on the notes of the Aberystwyth and Tregaron Bank Ltd, that had a motif of a sheep and a lamb and was widely accepted and known as The Black Sheep Bank.

PRIF TRYSORFA CYMRU CYFYNGEDIG
(CHIEF TREASURY OF WALES LIMITED)
LLANDUDNO, WALES

................................, 19........

Talwch
(Pay) ....

at ....

£ ....

Swm (ysgrifenwch yn lawn) ....
(Amount)

....

Cadeirydd ....

Richard Williams's first bills of exchange, issued in 1968, looked very similar to a conventional bank cheque of the period (below). Before issue to customers the bills were taxed with the blue embossed 2d stamp.

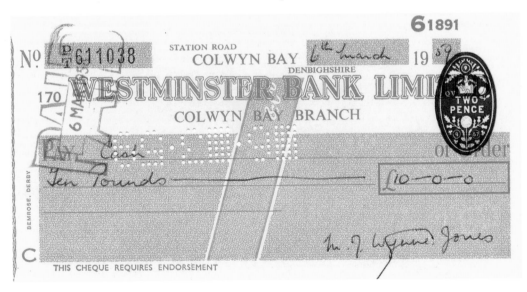

Williams's first £1 note depicted Caernarfon Castle on the reverse. This is one that the Government illegally endorsed with its 2d tax stamp.

The first one day after sight notes, initially with the Government's 2d tax stamp (above). The remainder were overprinted "Cancelled by Order" when the Government suppressed the name of the Chief Treasury of Wales.

When Williams issued his first 5-shilling notes the Welsh Black Cattle Society objected to the effeminacy of the bull ! Instead they authorised Williams to use their official bull symbol (below).

The design for the reverse of Williams's 5-shilling notes was a simple change of colour of the Japanese occupation currency note used in Malaya in World War Two.

Specimens of Williams's money that successfully passed through the national bank clearing system.

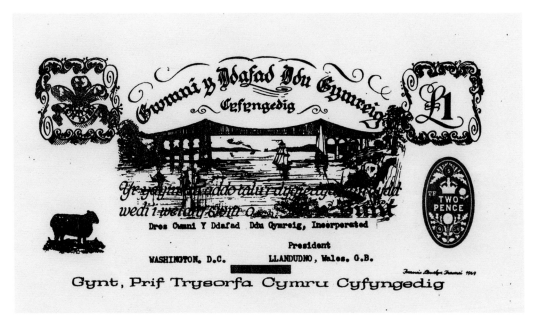

Williams's first American issue was endorsed with the British tax stamp. When the Government refused to stamp subsequent issues Williams legalised them by attaching a postage stamp – which at that time happened to be commemorating the National Giro Bank.

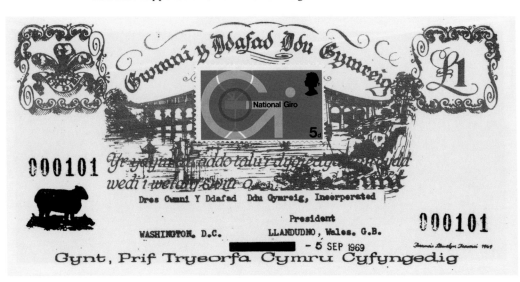

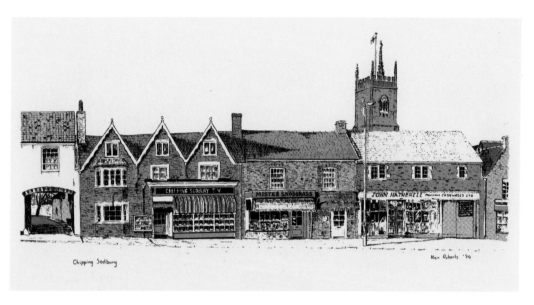

In 1985 Richard Williams re-emerged to issue £1 (above) and £5 (below) notes for Chipping Sodbury, in Avon. "I liked the name of the place," he said.

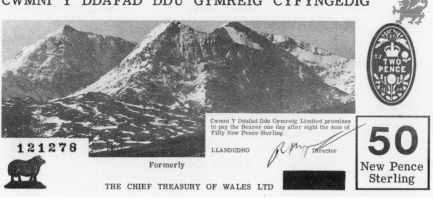

CWMNI Y DDAFAD DDU GYMREIG CYFYNGEDIG

121278

TWO PENCE

Cwmni Y Ddafad Ddu Gymreig Limited promises to pay the Bearer one day after sight the sum of Fifty New Pence Sterling

LLANDUDNO   Director

Formerly

THE CHIEF TREASURY OF WALES LTD

50
New Pence
Sterling

GREETINGS

50
New Pence
Sterling

Cymraeg for what was obviously a Welsh-language note, he was arguing that his notes issued in Wales were a separate currency, and therefore *Cymreig*. At last the lawyers at the Board of Inland Revenue had something to play with. On 3 November they returned a parcel of 1,000 unstamped notes to Mr. Williams, without explanation. *"My notes have been with them for a week, and apart from a letter asking me to translate the Welsh I have had no written explanation,"* he said.

"Quite apart from the folly of asking an interested party to supply his own translation, it is not my duty to supply Government departments with translations of Welsh documents. I am not a Welsh Nationalist but this kind of Government arrogance is enough to make any Welshman reconsider his position. It also highlights the need for a Stamp Office in North Wales," he said.

Upon trying to get an explanation from Somerset House, headquarters of the Board of Inland Revenue, he was told that everyone was acting under orders from the Controller of Stamps, at Bush House, who did not understand Welsh. *"I have failed in several attempts to contact the Controller of Stamps by telephone, and I await his explanation,"* said Williams. Meanwhile, at Somerset House, the spokesman told the author: *"We cannot discuss anyone's detailed affairs. In this case Mr. Williams knows our views,"* to which Williams retorted: *"I've no idea what they are talking about."*

A week later the Board of Inland Revenue wrote to Williams, saying they should never have stamped any of his home-made money. They said that way back in 1823, in the case of Jones versus Simpson, a judge had decided promissory notes must be for a definite sum, whereas Williams was promising to pay "not less than" their sterling equivalent. Furthermore, said the Inland Revenue, the Stamp Act of 1891 required promissory notes to be expressed in sterling or a foreign currency – and Mr. Williams maintained that his Welsh pounds were not sterling. A promissory note, said the Inland Revenue, must always be for a sum of money and, in 1899, a Queen's Bench judge defined money as that which passes freely from hand to hand throughout the community, in final discharge of debts and full payment for commodities, and without reference to the character or credit of the person who offers it. The notes that Mr. Williams had been printing since March did not comply with these requirements *"and therefore cannot be impressed with the Board's 2d duty stamp"*.

Richard Williams commented: *"I am disappointed that this is the best the Government's lawyers could come up with after eight months of research, and my voluminous correspondence with the Bank of England, Board of Trade and Board of Inland Revenue. Last March they tried to stop me by quoting a 1745 Act about window taxes in Berwick-upon-Tweed, but I got around that one. Since then they have stamped about 100,000 of my notes, which they now say they should never have done, and that amply illustrates their dilemma. They are at their wits' end trying to stop my issuing of Welsh pounds."*

Mr. Williams said he could easily bypass the British Government's lawyers by switching all his printing to his Washington-based company, which was headed by a prominent American lawyer. *"All I need do is have my Welsh pounds printed in the United States and shipped to Wales, where I can activate them simply by attaching a 2d postage stamp. That is the law and it will require an Act of Parliament to stop me. Furthermore, if the Board of Inland Revenue now says they taxed me in error 100,000 times I must be entitled to a refund. Because Wales is the only country in the world without its own banknotes my American colleagues envisage a Welsh dollar as the first truly international paper gold,"* he added.

In the meantime he successfully challenged the Government with a new note depicting Snowdon (copied from that year's Christmas card of local photographer John Lawson Reay) and inscribed "50 New Pence Sterling". It carried a new sheep design, being a photograph of an iron model given to him by the then famous

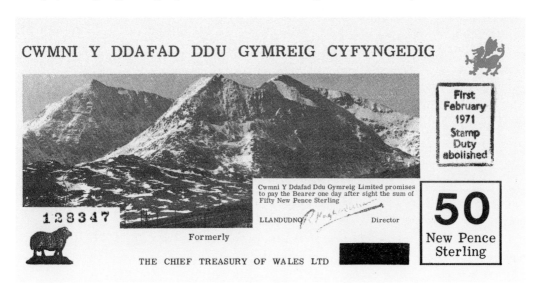

Welsh tourism entrepreneur and topographical print dealer Olwen Caradoc Evans. The reverse, printed in blue, carried a neat adaptation of the Japanese note, with vignettes of Caernarfon castle in each corner and the central legend "50 New Pence Sterling". He delivered 10,000 to the Manchester Stamp Office, where, despite the ruling of a few days earlier, they received the impressed 2d tax stamp on 27 November 1969.

His 50p note coincided with the launch of a 50 New Pence note by the Isle of Man Government, in response to the Bank of England's unpopular decision to withdraw the 10s note, and replace it with a heavy 50p coin on 14 October 1969, when it was actually worth 120 pence until the country switched to decimal currency on 15 February 1971.

Welcoming Richard Williams's initiative, Lord Langford, Constable of Rhuddlan Castle – where Royal currency was once minted – said: *"Our Manx cousins obviously have a lot more sense than the Decimal Currency Board."* He was president of the Anti-Heptagonists' Society, dedicated to the downfall of the 50p coin. *"A very kind official of the Finance Committee of the House of Keys sent me a Manx 50p note, advising me there were plenty more where that one came from, and saying he would be happy to receive my cheque,"* added Lord Langford.

Manx notes were in the exalted position of being legal tender in the Isle of Man, which was more than could be said for Scottish bank notes in Scotland. The Isle of Man never lost control over its own currency, and it was not until 1955 that the island decided to give Bank of England notes equal status. There is much confusion over the meaning of legal tender. In their November letter to Williams the Board of Inland Revenue had set out the rule of acceptability, not what constituted legal tender. At the present time the £1 coin is legal tender for any amount, and so presumably is the £2 coin. But the 50p and 20p coins may be used alone or in combination only up to a total tender of £10. The 10p and 5p coins are legal tender up to £5. The 2p and 1p coins are legal tender only up to 20p.

Chapter 5

Up your tabard!

Heraldry was the next weapon used by the Board of Inland Revenue in their war with Richard Williams. They telephoned him at the end of February 1970 saying he appeared to be making illegal use of the Royal Coat of Arms. In March they wrote saying: *"We have now been advised that the notes bear an heraldic device resembling the Arms of the Prince of Wales, which are part of the Royal Arms, and that the reproduction of the Royal Arms is subject to the authority of the office of the Lord Chamberlain. The general dispensation granted in 1969, to which you referred on the 'phone, has, we understand, now ceased, and in any event only applied to genuine souvenirs of the Investiture."*

Somerset House were somewhat out of their depth, in an intricate and colourful historical field that was not part of their remit. They were, of course, wrong in describing the famous three plumes within a coronet as the Arms of the Prince of Wales. The Arms, or shield, of the Prince is devoid of any feathers. The three plumes are a separate Royal "badge", usually reserved for use by each successive Prince of Wales, but sometimes used by Government to make special heraldic reference to Wales. It also appears in Welsh regimental and police badges.

"Do you intend to seek authority from the office of the Lord Chamberlain to use this device?" asked the Board of Inland Revenue. Williams's response was quick and simple. With the aid of a little metal polish he removed the two outer feathers from the printing plate for his 5s note, leaving behind a distinctly phallic-looking object. This was, of course, the note already adorned with a prize bull in all its masculine glory.

Gynt, Prif Trysorfa Cymru Cyfyngedig

"*They can read what they like into that,*" he said. "*The Government might prefer to see it as a silly little Red Indian feather, for there are people in London who seem to think Welshmen belong to some sort of Red Indian reservation. On the other hand my fellow Welshmen might think I am saying 'Up your tabard' to a charade of time-wasting humbug and an implied threat that the Lord Chamberlain will have me thrown into the Tower of London,*" added Richard Williams.

The Establishment appeared to go for the Red Indian option, perhaps believing Williams was smoking the pipe of peace. For whatever reason, London suddenly stopped harassing him. The destruction of the Britannia railway bridge by fire in May 1970 prompted Williams to issue a souvenir set of notes depicting the tubular bridge on the reverse and various locomotives of "the great little trains of Wales" on the front, in decimalised values of 20p, 50p, £1 and £2. They were overprinted "specimen" and never submitted for taxing, being intended only for the tourist trade. They were later described by Williams as "*a mistake, in retrospect, on the part of the Chief Treasury of Wales, for they cheapened what I was doing*".

In his April 1970 budget speech Chancellor of the Exchequer Roy Jenkins announced his proposed abolition of the 2d stamp duty on cheques and promissory notes, the following February. He attributed the abolition to the impending February switch to decimal currency, but those who had taken an interest in Richard Williams's operation saw it as a way of putting an end to his troublesome money. Mr. Jenkins told the House of Commons: "*The point that has weighed with me in regard to the cheque duty is that while it produces the useful revenue of £11m, to keep it would inevitably mean increasing the duty to one New Penny, an increase of 20%. There are at present probably at least 10m persons who hold bank accounts on which cheques can be drawn. The duty is thus an irritant which affects a great many people.*"

If Parliament had listened to the merchants of Caernarfon six decades earlier the

THE BLACK SHEEP COMPANY OF WALES LTD

Promises to pay the Bearer
one day after sight the sum of
TWENTY New Pence Sterling

R Hugh Williams
Director

20P

No. **SPECIMEN**

Formerly the
CHIEF TREASURY OF WALES LIMITED
Llandudno, Wales.

Tal-y-Llyn Railway

- 2 JUL 1971

upheaval of the change to decimal money would have long been over. Britain's first tentative step towards decimalisation was a disaster. It was in 1848, when silver florins were struck, at ten to the pound, and as a replacement for the half-crown (eight to the pound). The new florin omitted the initials DG, for *Dei Gratia* (by the Grace of God) after Queen Victoria's name, and the people were not slow to label it a Godless coin, unworthy of Christian usage. In 1856 a Royal Commission rejected any further decimalisation, and the minting of half-crowns was resumed, although the florin remained in use even into post-1971 decimalisation – when it was revalued at 10p.

In 1907 David Lloyd George, MP for Caernarfon Boroughs and President of the Board of Trade, was approached by W.A.Darbishire, the Mayor of Caernarfon, who thought the time was ripe for full continental style metrication. At a meeting of the Caernarfon Harbour Trust he successfully proposed that Parliament should be petitioned accordingly. That same evening he repeated his proposition at a meeting of the Borough Council. Seconding the motion, Dr. Robert Parry said he did so in the interests of the coming generation and in the knowledge that a lot of time had been wasted learning the existing anomalous system. A note of caution was sounded by Councillor John T.Roberts (Lloyd George's first election agent) who said a metric system would cause great hardship to shopkeepers, who would have to replace all their weights.

A Council resolution was sent to Lloyd George, soon to become Chancellor of the Exchequer, but he had many more pressing problems to attend to. The idea lay dormant on Lloyd George's desk until 1918 when, as Prime Minister, he set up a Royal Commission to examine the whole question of decimalisation. However he did not challenge the Commission's subsequent report, which rejected any change.

As decimalisation loomed nearer Richard Williams decided to test the water with two prototype designs for £1 and £2 notes, which he sent to Somerset House in December. They were taxed without comment, bearing the 2d duty stamp incorporating the date 7.12.70. Before the week was out he despatched a new decimal set of notes which were taxed on 14 December, despite carrying the historically rebellious words: *"This Welsh Note is one of a special set of one hundred of a new issue made to anticipate decimalisation in Great Britain, and the abolition of Stamp Duty on all promissory notes from 1st February 1971. It has been left untrimmed and stamped on the offcut to confirm the authenticity and acceptance by the British Government of these notes and their legal negotiability."*

They were illustrated with portraits of famous Welshmen, and their values were fractionalised rather than decimalised, although readily recognisable for either use. The 5s note was inscribed *"£ CHWARTER"*, (meaning *"£-quarter"*) and described as promising to pay *"y swm o Goron"*, (*"the sum of a crown."*). The 10s note was inscribed *"£ HANER"* (£-half), and promised to pay *"Chweugain"*. Now obsolete, the term *"chweugain"* was always used in pre-decimal currency days for the 10s note. The word was an abbreviation of *"chwe ugain ceiniog"*, meaning "six

Cwmni y Ddafad Ddu Gymreig
Cyfyngedig

£ CHWARTER

Yr ydym un addo talu'r dygiedydd un dydd
wedi'i weld y swm o...... GORON

Dros Cwmni Y Ddafad Ddu Gymreig Limited

LLANDUDNO Cyfarwyddwr

-1 FEB 1971

SIR JOHN TREVOR.

No. 892453

Gynt, Prif Trysorfa Cymru Cyfyngedig

Cwmni y Ddafad Ddu Gymreig
Cyfyngedig

£ UN

Yr ydym un addo talu'r dygiedydd un dydd
wedi'i weld y swm o...... UN BUNT

Dros Cwmni Y Ddafad Ddu Gymreig Limited

LLANDUDNO Cyfarwyddwr

-1 FEB 1971

HUMPHREY LLWYD.

No. 893498

Gynt, Prif Trysorfa Cymru Cyfyngedig

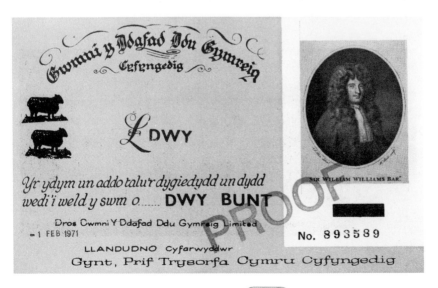

Cwmni y Ddafad Ddu Gymreig
Cyfyngedig

£ DWY

Yr ydym un addo talu'r dygiedydd un dydd
wedi'i weld y swm o...... DWY BUNT

Dros Cwmni Y Ddafad Ddu Gymreig Limited
-1 FEB 1971

LLANDUDNO Cyfarwyddwr

SIR WILLIAM WILLIAMS BAR.

No. 893589

Gynt, Prif Trysorfa Cymru Cyfyngedig

times twenty pennies", i.e. 120 pence, which was half the 240d in the pre-1971 pound. The other notes were for £1 and £2. They initially carried illustrations of Judge George Jeffreys (5s), Sir John Vaughan (10s), Humphrey Llwyd (£1) and Sir William Williams (£2). A woman objected to the inclusion of Judge Jeffreys, of Wrexham, because of his notoriety for presiding over what came to be known as the Bloody Assizes, during which he sentenced hundreds to hang after the Duke of Monmouth's rebellion of 1685. Williams obliged by issuing a replacement note featuring Sir John Trevor.

"These are definitely my last notes," said Williams on 12 February 1971, three days before Britain switched to decimal currency – but they were not, as we were to discover 14 years later! Having lost the prestigious endorsement of the crowned 2d tax stamp, and with the various Government departments having retreated behind their London desks, Richard Williams decided he had won the battle, although he was disappointed that no Welsh politicians had taken up his war cry for a Welsh pound.

"I see no purpose in printing any more Welsh money," he said. *"You will recall that was never the prime reason for my establishing the Chief Treasury of Wales. The unexpectedly popular notes were largely a coincidental development from my main contest with the world's clearing banks, all of which are using my encoding system without paying me anything for it,"* he told the author.

However he had not given up the greater vision of Wales's playing an important part in shaping international trade. *"By creating a Welsh pound outside the fetters of sterling control imposed on the former British Empire I hoped to show that one could use a common currency for use by trading nations across the world. It would be far too difficult to sit the delegates of a hundred nations around a table and*

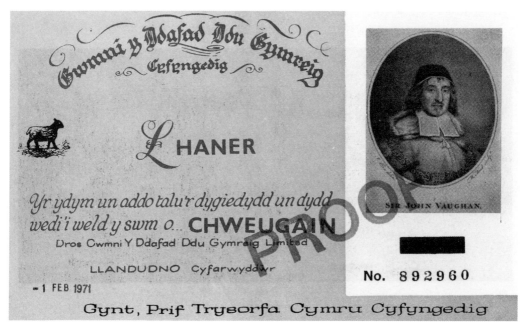

expect them to agree an international currency by negotiation. But I believe a small country like Wales, or Monaco, or Luxembourg could play an important role.

"For that to happen it only needs a nation with a universally-desired commodity to say it wants to trade in Welsh pounds. That would result in Welsh pounds coming into use on a universal scale. It is only necessary for one of the Middle East oil producing nations to demand payment in Welsh pounds to cause Welsh pounds to circulate as an international currency. Instead of paper money being backed by gold, as it used to be – and still purports to be – it could be backed by the much more valuable black gold, the oil of Arabia," said Richard Williams.

It would be foolish, he said, to imagine that Middle East oil producers would fall in with such a scheme unless they owned the Chief Treasury of Wales, or its successor, the Welsh Black Sheep "Bank". As this was a privately owned company there was no reason why a Middle Eastern country should not buy a majority or total holding – and he was open to offers.

"Already Iran has established its own stock exchange, and all the Middle East oil producers are embarrassed by their wealth, with which they are acquiring assets in the developing countries, including Great Britain," he said – and he did not have to wait long for a flattering response and a vision of mega-wealth.

In 1971 Williams was approached by an accountant from Woolhampton, with a £5m offer of investment from the Shah of Iran, jointly with two Arab oil sheiks, Prince Michael of Yugoslavia, a leading firm of merchant bankers, and Christopher Shawcross, QC, who would look after the legal side. The matter proceeded via a series of telephone conversations (which Williams recorded), in one of which the accountant said he had just flown into London in the Shah's private jet, which the Shah would be sending to Heathrow in four weeks time, to fly Williams to Teheran for further negotiations.

That was the strange story told to Judge Meurig Evans at Llandudno County Court, on 8 March 1973, when Richard Williams asked for an award of £686 incurred in visiting and entertaining the 47-years-old accountant in a costly suite he had hired at a Heathrow hotel.

"It does not look as though you have got a leg to stand on," interjected the judge, adding: "I advise you to go and see a solicitor before wasting any more of your valuable time pursuing a useless claim."

"The issue is a little more complicated than that," replied Williams. "So far as I have been able to ascertain, Prince Michael of Yugoslavia does not exist. I visited the Iranian Embassy in London and saw an assistant to the Ambassador who told me the Shah did not own a private jet, in which the defendant is supposed to have visited Teheran to discuss the matter. Mr. Shawcross denies any connection with the defendant. It may sound as though I have been gullible but the defendant was extremely – what shall I say..."

"Plausible," interjected the judge, saying Williams would be foolish if he did not accept his earlier advice and go and see someone who knew something about the law. "*You are sailing in uncharted waters. I shall adjourn this case to next month to give you an opportunity to take legal advice,*" he added. The accused accountant rose to say he might not be available in a month's time, to which the judge replied: "*I advise you, as I have advised the plaintiff, to go and see a solicitor.*"

When the hearing was resumed on 12 April, Williams – who was still presenting his own case – described how he had waited in vain at a Heathrow hotel suite for an appointment with the Shah of Persia. But no one turned up and nobody at Heathrow seemed to know anything about the Shah's aircraft. The Iranian Embassy later told him the Shah did not hobnob with Arab sheiks, and would not have contemplated a conference such as Mr. Williams had been waiting for. "*I do not pretend to know what is behind all this, but I am out of pocket on it,*" he pleaded.

The defendant did not put in an appearance at the adjourned hearing and he was not represented. Dismissing the case, Judge Evans said: "*The claim came before me at Llandudno last month when I advised the plaintiff to seek legal advice on the preparation of his claim. He tells me this morning that the firm of solicitors whom he saw fit to consult could teach him nothing at all about the law and procedure necessary to substantiate his claim.*

"*He has given evidence this morning and if half of what he says is true he has shown himself to be one of the most gullible of people and the defendant has shown himself to be a somewhat plausible person. However interesting the story is, that he has told this morning, one thing is certain: it reveals no basis for a claim of any sort. Apparently the defendant told the plaintiff he was in a position to obtain substantial money for investment. On the basis of that the plaintiff was foolish enough to incur travelling expenses without checking what this plausible person had to say, and in these circumstances the loss falls entirely on him,*" concluded the judge.

Richard Williams had been told that so far as the Bank of England was concerned his *Punt Gymreig,* or Welsh Pound, meant nothing more than an English pound sterling. The pound unit of currency came to Wales from England, after the medieval settlement in London of the Lombards. It was they who brought with them the £ or L symbol, as an abbreviation of the Latin word *libra,* meaning a pound weight. Its adoption as a unit of currency was derived from Charlemagne (or Carolus), founder of the Holy Roman Empire, who decided in 793 AD that 240 *deniers* should be made from a pound weight of silver. By the time the money lenders from Lombardy settled in London 240 silver pennies weighed the same as a pound (1-lb, or one *libra*) of sterling silver – although the first £1 coin was a gold sovereign weighing 240 grains, issued in 1489, during the reign of Henry VII, and exchangeable for 20 shillings. The first coin actually designated a "pound" was struck in gold, during the reign of Queen Elizabeth I. A silver pound was struck for Charles I (1625-49). In Scotland, however, the monetary pound was equivalent to only one-twelfth of £1 sterling, i.e. 1s 8d of English currency. By way of further confusion both the English and the Scottish pounds were divided into twenty shillings, so that a Scottish shilling was worth only one English penny, while an English shilling (first struck in 1504) comprised twelve English pennies – right up to the decimalisation of British coins in 1971. The first Scottish pound coin, called "twenty shillings", was issued in the reign of Queen Mary (1542-67). Scottish *nobles, merks, placks, ryals, units, dollars, pistoles, bodies* and *bawbees* were to emerge before the Act of Union of 1707.

In the 1971 decimalisation of British currency the pound sterling survived intact. Until then pounds, shillings and pence were abbreviated as £-s-d. However the "s" was not derived directly from *shilling* but from the Roman *solidus aureus,* originally a gold coin struck by Constantine the Great. He was probably the garrison commander at Segontium (Caernarfon) in 306, guarding the rich mineral wealth of North Wales, including gold and silver, before riding off to Rome to execute his reigning brother-in-law and seize the throne. His innovative coin later became the *solidus argenteus,* or silver *solidus.* The shilling disappeared in the

1971 decimalisation. The name *penny* survived, but its old "d" abbreviation, derived from the Roman *denarius*, was replaced by "p", originally for "new pence" and after 1982 for "pence". Much to the annoyance of language purists, the full word "pence" is now rarely spoken. When the Romans arrived in Britain a soldier's daily rate of pay was one *denarius,* and there were 25d in one *aureus* – not very different from the 24 halfpennies in a British shilling in 1971. Inflation is not a new phenomenon and by 215 AD the legionary's pay was 675d per annum.

Imperial Rome closed its London mint in 325 but it was briefly reopened in 383 by Magnus Maximus, the Spanish-born senior commander of the forces in Britain, after he had declared himself emperor in the west, with his capital at Trier. He was killed after invading Italy in 388, but not before he had established a permanent niche in Welsh legend as the Emperor Macsen Wledig (i.e. Magnus the Ruler). One of the eleven ancient stories of the *Mabinogion,* first written down between 1300 and 1325, tells of the emperor's fulfilling a dream by sailing into the mouth of the River Seiont, at Caernarfon, to the fort of Segontium, to sleep with the virgin Helen. Like Constantine before him, legend has it that it was from Caernarfon that he set off for Rome. He has left us his likeness on two of his British coins, the *denarius* and the *sestertius.*

The pound remains as a unit of currency across the world, in countries that came under British influence, such as Egypt, Cyprus, Malta, Falkland Islands, Gibraltar, Sudan, Lebanon and Syria (the latter having traded with British mandated Palestine and Transjordan). It was used in Israel from political independence (and initial use of the Palestine pound devalued against sterling) in 1948 until the adoption of the *shekel* in 1980, to try to mask soaring inflation with an exchange of 1 *shekel* for 10 Israeli pounds. When translated into Gaelic as the *punt,* the pound was used in the Republic of Ireland until the adoption of the *euro* in 2002. Reverting to its Latin origins, the *lira* was the Italian unit of currency, using the £ symbol, until the advent of the *euro.* The *lira* remains in use in Turkey, although usually referred to as the pound, using the £ symbol.

Countless discoveries tell us Roman and a few pre-Roman coins were widely used in Wales. After the departure of the Romans in 409 the use of coins appears to have ceased for more than a century. Subsequently Wales probably used the coinage in the borderlands derived from trade with neighbouring England. Most bizarre of these coins would be those made for King Offa, of Mercia (757-96), famous for his wall and ditch, still traceable from Prestatyn, on the North Wales coast, to Monmouth in the South, and known as Offa's Dyke. It marked the western frontier of his kingdom, seemingly agreed by negotiation rather than conquest (and west of the present boundary). His gold coins were inscribed in Arabic, being copies of the Baghdad *dinar* of the Iraqi Abbasid Caliph Al-Mansur. They bore the Arabic date *IOV*, i.e. the Islamic calendar year 157, being the 157th anniversary of Muhammad's migration from Mecca to Madina (*Anno Hegirae*). AH 157 was 774 AD, and was only one year after Al-Mansur set up his Islamic capital in Baghdad, from where the Abbasids, taking their name from the Prophet Muhammad's uncle Abbas, continued to reign until the city was sacked by the Mongols in 1258 AD. One wonders why Offa chose this unmistakably Arab design, from the faraway ruling centre of Islam, and how it reached the Welsh borders so soon after its issue in Baghdad. His name OFFA REX (King Offa) was inscribed in Latin on the reverse. He also struck coins of indigenous design bearing a portrait and the name of his wife, CYNEDRID REGIN, at a time when TH was rendered as D, i.e. Cynedrid Regin[a] = Queen Cynethryth, a name of British construction and probably Welsh. Pennies bearing a portrait of Offa were minted at Canterbury, much of the design being copied from the Roman *siliqua* of Julian II, minted at Trier.

Oddly, Wales does not appear to have had its own currency, with the exception of the reign of Howel Dda, c916-950. Only one coin is known to have survived, perhaps because of subsequent smelting for re-use. It is made of gold and inscribed HOPEL REX, with a small cross on the obverse, and the moneyer's (manufacturer's) name in two lines, and with crosses, on the reverse, suggesting it was probably made in Chester. In Anglo-Saxon and Norman times the letter W was frequently rendered to look like P – coins for William the Conqueror were inscribed "PILELLMUS". Thus HOPEL REX reads as King Howel. The conventional Welsh form Howel Dda means Howel the Good.

While Wales did not have its own currency there were Norman mints in the country. Their coins are identifiable by their mint marks. CAIRDI (reign of William I, 1066-87), CARDI (reign of Henry I, 1100-35) and CARITI (reign of Stephen, 1135-54) were used for coins made at Cardiff, then an insignificant former Roman town on the banks of the Taff, but now the capital of Wales. Visitors to today's little town of Rhuddlan, in North Wales, might be surprised to learn it was minting coins for William the Conqueror, using the mint marks RVDILI and RVLA (when U was represented by V). The mint was probably located in the motte and bailey castle built in 1073, much of which still stands south-east of the more prominent castle of Edward I. Pembroke used the mint marks PAN and PAIN for coins made for Henry I.

Silver from Welsh mines was widely used for coinage. Towards the end of the reign of James I (1603-25) coins made of Welsh silver were marked by three plumes within a coronet, in the distinctive design still well known as the badge of the Prince of Wales. The coin designs sometimes featured the feathers above the royal arms, and sometimes they were placed alone behind the monarch mounted on a horse.

In 1637 a royal branch mint was set up at Aberystwyth Castle to make coins out of Welsh silver for Charles I. The mint had to be financed by Thomas Bushell, who had petitioned for its establishment as an alternative to sending Cardiganshire silver to London for minting. The dies were supplied from London, to make denominations comprising the double-crown, crown, half-crown, unite, shilling, sixpence, three-pence, half-groat and penny. The castle was badly damaged by the Parliamentary troops during the Civil War and the mint was moved to Ysgubor-y-coed, with the intention of returning to the castle after it had been repaired, but that was never achieved.

Although the former Aberystwyth mint was not used for the coinage of Charles II, after the restoration of the monarchy, the Prince of Wales's feathers were incorporated in the design of coins struck in London from Welsh silver during his reign. By a strange coincidence the Aberystwyth mint mark was an open book, in the town where the National Library of Wales was to be established nearly three centuries later.

A shortage of small denomination coins prompted the widespread use of privately minted traders' tokens from about 1613. The copper penny issued by Conwy grocer Henry Hughes in 1663 seems to be the oldest surviving Welsh specimen. Others have turned up right across the country, including the undated pennies of Holyhead innkeepers J.Wheldon and William Owen, and the 1665 penny of a Ruthin apothecary. This batch of tokens fell into disuse after 1672 when the Royal Mint was ordered to produce its first copper coins, halfpennies and farthings. Like their silver predecessors, the copper coins contained metal matching their face value, and were therefore unpopular because of their weight and cost of transportation.

Standard currency was not minted every year. Apart from a farthing issued in 1714, no copper coins were minted during the reign of Queen Anne (1702-14), and the only silver pennies issued were in 1703, 1705-6, 1708-10 and 1713. There was a reasonable supply of low-value coins for George I (1714-27), but few were minted during the reign of George II (1727-60), and few coins of any denomination during the latter half of the 18th century. Various ruses were used to make up the shortage, including the stamping of a small impression of the head of George III on Spanish-American silver 8-*reales* coins ("pieces-of-eight") worth 4s 9d. The Bank of England (whose remit is to issue paper money, not coins) issued re-struck 8-*reales* in 1804, portraying George III on the obverse, with Britannia on the reverse and the inscription "Bank of England Five shillings dollar". The bank also issued emergency money during 1811-16, showing the king's head on the obverse but marked on the reverse with the words "Bank token 3 shill", "Bank token 1s 6d" and "Bank token 9d".

It was against that background of shortage in low-value regal coinage that the Parys Mine Company, at Amlwch, in Anglesey, started a rash of new token issues across Britain in 1787. The Amlwch mines produced copper ore which, when

blended with the slightly different ores of the Great Orme mines at Llandudno, kept the Swansea smelters busy. With plenty of copper available, Thomas Williams, a lawyer and managing partner of the Parys Mine Company, commissioned his famous design from William Collins, of Greenwich, for die engraver John Milton, of London. A druid's head is shown on the obverse, while the reverse design embraces the entwined cipher *PMCo*, and words "we promise to pay the bearer one penny", plus the capitalised initial "D" (*denarius*) and date. Around the edge of the token were the words "on demand in London, Liverpool, Anglesey". They were well-made at Williams's Greenfield Valley works at Holywell, in Flintshire. Subsequent issues, including a halfpenny of matching design (but inscribed "The Anglesey Mines halfpenny"), were struck at Williams's new mint in Birmingham, and by Matthew Boulton after his 1789 purchase of the plant. Each strike was slightly different in detail but the fundamental design remained the same. The Anglesey coins were minted until 1791 and became widely used across Britain. Their acceptability was such that there were several counterfeits in circulation.

Hard on the heels of Thomas Williams's enterprise, his business associate John Wilkinson, of the Bersham Ironworks, Brymbo, near Wrexham, began issuing tokens, initially both silver and copper halfpennies. They appeared with the dates 1788, 1790, 1792 and 1793. They were adorned with a likeness of Wilkinson on the obverse and the legend "John Wilkinson Iron Master" on the reverse. Different issues were inscribed around the edge, "Anglesey, London or Liverpool", "Bersham, Bradley, Willey, Snedhill", "Payable at London or Anglesey", and "At Birmingham, Brighton or Liverpool". The 1788 issue was decorated with a French harp surmounted by a crown, and the words "North Wales". In December 1792 John Wilkinson began issuing pioneering printed promissory notes for one guinea. He died in 1808 but his executors were issuing "Brymbo Ironworks" guinea notes until at least 1814.

A crowned harp was also used on a coin inscribed "North Wales Token 1797" on one side, and "S.Roberts, Ironmonger, Bangor" on the other. The Prince of

Wales's feathers adorned a farthing token issued in Pembroke in 1793, and inscribed "Medallion of St.David". The earliest known monetary use of the Welsh language was on a Glamorgan halfpenny depicting Britannia on one side, with the words "Y Brenin ar Gyfraith Ex 1795" (meaning The King and the Law), while the other side carried the words "Iestyn ap Gwrgan, Tywysog Morganwg 1091" (Iestyn son of Gwrgan, Prince of Glamorgan 1091). Hadrian was the first to decorate coins with the now very familiar symbol of a woman, and the word BRITANNIA. There were numerous other issues of tokens across Wales.

Ironically, it was to Llantrisant, in South Wales, that the Royal Mint moved in 1968, to begin manufacturing the coins for decimalisation in 1971. The Queen officially opened the Welsh Mint in 1969, while Richard Williams was busily creating his Welsh pound notes at Llandudno, 200 miles to the north. The official opening coincided with the release of the first 50p coin, designed to replace the 10s note. It was inscribed "new pence" and was very much bigger and heavier than the present 50p coin.

Wales was represented in the new coinage by the Prince of Wales's feathers on the reverse of the 2p coin. Coins for £1 were issued in 1983, to replace the Bank of England's £1 note. Two years later the Government seemed to adopt, without fuss, Williams's 1969 plea for a Welsh pound. The 1985 issue of £1 coins featured the Welsh leek, and carried the Welsh inscription around the edge: *Pleidiol wyf i'm gwlad*, meaning "faithful am I to my country", taken from a line in the Welsh national anthem *Hen wlad fy nhadau*. The same inscription around the edge was retained when the 1995 £1 coin was issued, featuring the Welsh dragon, from the flag of Wales, *Y ddraig goch*.

Chapter 7

What price a Bank of Wales?

Central to the 1968 registration of Williams's Chief Treasury of Wales Ltd. was his interest in preserving the integrity of the prestigious title of Bank of Wales. It will be recalled that the finance panel of the new Welsh Economic Advisory Council was then investigating the need for such a financial institution. He raised his concern in letters to the Prime Minister and the Board of Trade, the latter assuring him *"no company would be registered with the name of Bank of Wales Ltd unless the Board considered this fully justified".* Williams promptly formed his £100 company Prif Trysorfa Cymru Ltd., translating as Chief Treasury of Wales, and proceeded to tell various Government departments that this had rendered the establishment of a Bank of Wales unnecessary.

On 27 September 1968 Mr. G.B.Diamond, private secretary to the Secretary of State for Wales, wrote to Mr. Williams saying: *"As you may know, the problem of facilities in Wales for finance to industry, including the question of a possible Bank of Wales, is currently being examined by the Finance Panel of the Welsh Council under the chairmanship of Professor Brinley Thomas. The Secretary of State expects in due course to be receiving a report from the Council setting out their views on these matters. In the meantime he is arranging for your letter to be brought to the attention of the Finance Panel."*

By return Williams wrote to the Prime Minister's private secretary, D.H.Andrews, at 10 Downing Street, saying Mr. Diamond's letter from the London office of the Welsh Office added a great deal of fuel to the flames. *"I am more than ready to believe Mr. Diamond just would not understand what all the fuss might be about...I seriously doubt if the Secretary of State for Wales or the Prime Minister personally have seen any of the correspondence. I have never heard of Professor Brinley Thomas, any more than perhaps he has of me, but I should be interested to know what statutory executive power his Finance Panel, or indeed the Welsh Council, has in these matters."* With his ear close to the ground in the matter of Cardiff political gossip about the machinations within the city's ruling Socialist fraternity, Williams warned the Prime Minister's office that there were people who intended to act while the Government's Welsh Council talked.

The answering letter came not from Downing Street, but from the Welsh Office, at 47 Parliament Street, and was personally signed by Secretary of State George Thomas, on 16 October. He said: *"I can assure you there is the closest liaison between the Board of Trade and the Welsh Office on the question of the use of the name Bank of Wales, and that we are fully aware of the implications of the adoption of that name.*

"You say in your letter of 29 September that you have never heard of Professor Brinley Thomas. He is, in fact, the chairman of the Welsh Council, as well as being

chairman of the Council's Finance Panel. He is also an internationally renowned economist. The Welsh Council was appointed by the Government to advise on a wide range of topics. Specific subjects are examined by panels or committees of the Council, and the question of a Bank of Wales is being considered by the Finance Panel as part of a more comprehensive study of the availability of finance for industrial development in Wales."

Williams replied to George Thomas on 1 November, saying that as the Chief Treasury of Wales was already in existence, *"any discussion by you and your colleagues on the formation of a possible Bank of Wales is now unnecessary."*

For their all-important denouement of their Bank of Wales project the Welsh Council chose to meet at Richard Williams's home town of Llandudno – for their first ever meeting in North Wales. Was that intended as a coded message to Williams? All but five of the 36 members spent two days at the St. George's Hotel, on 20 and 21 April, in the presence of Welsh Office Minister of State Mrs. Eirene White, MP. The Council met in camera to discuss a report from their Finance Panel but at the end of the session Professor Thomas told the author, during a recorded interview, that the need for a privately financed Bank of Wales had been recognised, adding: *"The initiative does not rest with us or the Government."*

"If some private source should put up a viable proposal for registration of a Bank of Wales then we would ask the authorities concerned to have full and sympathetic regard for the views of the Welsh Council," said Professor Thomas, adding that his finance panel had spent eight or nine months considering whether Wales needed the kind of financial institution arising out of the argument that small and medium sized firms encountered lots of difficulties in raising capital for long term expansion. They had interviewed various witnesses from the financial world and had also looked at the experience of small countries such as Eire, Canada and Scotland.

"We came to the conclusion, by a big majority of the panel, that there was a case for such an institution, bearing in mind the needs of Wales to increase its rate of resource utilisation and economic growth. It was felt there was a need for a means of mobilising small deposits to provide a flexible supply of capital for long-term investment, as distinct from bridging loans, which are the function of existing merchant banks.

"By being an institution with an exclusive commitment to Wales, and as a recognised Welsh institution capable of assessing and projecting the needs of Wales in the wider financial world, it would also attract a flow of foreign deposits, helping to overcome the relative scarcity of Welsh resources. It would also provide an adequate channel to promote new investment for foreign countries in Wales, since bankers do play an important part in foreign investment," said Professor Thomas.

He said it was not within the Council's terms of reference to go into the mechanics of bringing a Bank of Wales into effect. There were no precedents for such a complex proposal and he could not think of any existing English institution comparable with what the panel thought necessary for Wales. Having arrived at a resolution it was not very clear what they should do with it, he said. The Council would be reporting to the Secretary of State for Wales, George Thomas, but Professor Thomas said he would like to make it clear that the financial backing for such an institution would have to come from a private source.

Asked if he could be more explicit about the kind of Bank of Wales the Council had in mind, Professor Thomas replied they could not, apart from pointing out that they were not talking about a note-issuing institution. *"Its major function would be to promote long-term investment,"* he added.

Cardiff merchant banker Julian Hodge, one of the members of the Welsh Council meeting at Llandudno, told the author that proposals for a Bank of Wales, with an initial capital of £5m, were already with the Board of Trade. *"A Bank of Wales would be a symbol of regional development attracting funds from within the Principality and from outside, for reinvestment in Wales in order to help indigenous industry, and urgently quicken the pace of diversification,"* said Mr. Hodge. Such a bank would attract foreign investment, giving Wales the benefit of cheaper money that could often be obtained overseas easier than the dearer and restricted supply from within Britain.

"As a financial focal point of the Welsh economy, a Bank of Wales would have the opportunity, through its contacts overseas – with particular reference to the United States – to be able to influence direct investment into the Principality and thus directly attract new industries," said Mr. Hodge. If Wales were to expand at only half the rate of Scottish expansion during the previous twenty years the whole economy of the Principality would change rapidly, he said.

How soon could one expect to see such a Bank of Wales opening its doors for business? asked the author. Mr. Hodge replied: *"A memorandum of articles of association for the formation of a company to be called Bank of Wales Ltd., with an initial capital of £5m, was submitted to the authorities some two months ago. The matter is now with the Board of Trade and the Bank of England. If the Bank of Wales is to succeed in the high purpose envisaged it must have the support of the authorities and the blessing of the Bank of England, and possibly the joint stock banks."* He said his new bank would not be involved in note issuing activities, *"at least not for the foreseeable future."*

Three days later, on 24 April, Julian Hodge addressed the annual luncheon of the Welsh branch of the Institute of Directors, at which the author was present, in the Park Hotel, Cardiff. He said Wales was the only constituent country of the United Kingdom without a recognisably indigenous bank, apart from his own merchant bank bearing his name.

Noting that his Llandudno announcement about his proposed Bank of Wales had sparked off a lot of interest, Mr. Hodge said its policy would be decided in a way that was relevant to Welsh needs. The economic depression of the 1930s had a devastating effect in Wales because of the failure to diversify and develop indigenous Welsh industries. Wales needed its own investment bank to give greater stimulus to the development of indigenous industry.

"*It would be fair to say, perhaps, that financial institutions which operate in Wales only marginally, and have their main business elsewhere, will have their board policies decided by criteria that may not always be relevant to Welsh needs,*" he said, adding that the banks of Ireland or Scotland, although operating to a limited extent outside their own countries, stood or fell by their record in Ireland or Scotland. Similarly a Bank of Wales would have to succeed in Wales. It would have no alibi and neither would it need one, given the dynamism already shown in Wales and the likely and necessary increase in Welsh industrial growth.

"*Let me say, straight away, in case there should be any misunderstanding, the Bank of Wales, as I see it, would be a profit-making undertaking,*" Mr. Hodge told his audience, who would be expected to provide much of the capital for the proposed venture. "*Our new bank must be profitable and be seen to make profits, otherwise it cannot, in its turn, attract the capital or deposits it would need for the investment I have described. It would need to attract deposits from Wales and the United Kingdom, and from overseas. Indeed I think it would attract a great deal of investment saving in South Wales, and stop what I believe is the net outflow of capital from the Principality.*"

Essentially, said Mr. Hodge, the Bank of Wales should be an investment bank concentrating on helping and advising the promotion of healthy development. Diversification of Welsh industry compared unfavourably with any other region of Britain. Moreover, he said, a large proportion of the working population of Wales was in undertakings controlled from outside Wales, which he saw as an economically dangerous situation.

"*I am not suggesting, surprisingly enough, that the Bank of Wales should be a note-issuing bank. That, in my opinion, is not part of the main purpose for which the bank should be established, although some will argue that if nothing else, a Welsh bank note could be good for the tourist trade,*" said Mr. Hodge.

The main aim of the Bank of Wales should be to build up Cardiff as a financial centre that would at least be equal to anything in Scotland, and begin to compare with what was best anywhere in the world, added Mr. Hodge – who was knighted the following year.

Meeting in Cardiff on 10 December, the Welsh Regional Council of the Confederation of British Industry declared its unanimous support for Mr. Hodge's proposed Bank of Wales – although quick to hedge its bets by saying this did not imply any criticism of the work of the existing joint stock banks.

Perhaps Richard Williams's protests about preserving the prestigious title of Bank of Wales, and his quest for Welsh bank notes, had something to do with the Government's decision to approve the somewhat less impressive name of Commercial Bank of Wales Ltd. for the company incorporated on 9 February 1971, with a capital of £100. On 10 October 1972 the authorised share capital was increased to £7,500,000, in £1 shares, and on 17 October the company published its prospectus and invited applications for shares.

Its list of founder directors read like a Cardiff Who's Who. They were Socialist millionaire and former railway clerk Sir Julian Hodge, chairman (with a personal holding of 100,000 shares), former Chancellor of the Exchequer and future Prime Minister The Rt.Hon. James Callaghan (1,000), former Permanent Secretary at the Welsh Office and newly-appointed Principal of the University College of Wales Sir Goronwy Daniel (5,000), Recorder of Cardiff Alun Talfan Davies, QC (10,000), William A.Ellis (5,000), The Rt.Hon. Lord Harlech (10,000), John Hoddell (5,000), Homer J.Livingston, Jr. of Chicago (none), Gordon J.Sapstead (none), Samuel E.Taylor (5,000), The Rt.Hon. George Thomas, Speaker of the House of Commons (1,000), Lord Lieutenant of Glamorgan Sir Cennydd Traherne (5,000) and F.Donald Walters (5,000).

Corporate shareholders were listed as: Charterhouse Japhet Ltd (£100,000), Clive Discount Company Ltd (£50,000), First Chicago Ltd., a subsidiary of the First National Bank of Chicago (£1,000,000), Friends' Provident & Century Life Office (£100,000), Gerrard & National Discount Co.Ltd. (£50,000), Hambros Bank (Nominees) Ltd. (£100,000), Harmsworth Pension Fund (£50,000), Hodge General & Mercantile Insurance Co.Ltd. (£48,000), Hodge Group Ltd. (£250,000), Hodge Life Assurance Co.Ltd. (£250,000), HTV Ltd. (£200,000), Julian S.Hodge & Co.Ltd. (£250,000), Sir William Reardon Smith & Sons Ltd. (£100,000), Smith St.Aubyn & Co.Ltd. (£50,000), South Wales Argus Ltd. (£50,000) and Sun Alliance & London Insurance Ltd. (£200,000).

There were those who questioned the Welshness of a Cardiff bank in which an American bank held a 20% holding and a seat on the board, while North Wales had no direct representation, but the offer of shares was nine times oversubscribed. The Commercial Bank of Wales opened for business on 30 October 1972, at 114-116 St.Mary Street. Hodge made it clear from the outset that he looked forward to the day he could delete the word "Commercial" from the bank's title. On the eve of the bank's opening Sir Julian described how he had enlisted the backing of the First National Bank of Chicago, who already had some clients in South Wales. He set his sights on Gaylord Freeman, president of the Chicago bank when it hosted International Monetary Fund delegates in Washington, in 1971, and told him about his forthcoming Bank of Wales. Next morning First Chicago's overseas investment executive called on Sir Julian at the Shoreham Hotel, at 7 a.m. for a working breakfast. *"By nine o'clock it was agreed in principle,"* said Sir Julian.

Richard Williams was not the only Welsh entrepreneur to do battle with the Bank of England. At the May 1981 annual general meeting of shareholders of the Commercial Bank of Wales, in Cardiff's Park Hotel, Sir Julian Hodge said the name "bank" would have to be dropped from the title by January 1982, unless they were successful in their appeal against the refusal of full banking status. He said he was bewildered by the Bank of England ruling, under the Banking Act, 1979, especially since the appeal was not scheduled for hearing until the autumn of 1983. He said the Commercial Bank of Wales would be presenting evidence from its customers to demonstrate to the tribunal the wide range and efficient banking services provided.

"*When you recall that we were set up with the full approval of the Bank of England, the Treasury, the then Board of Trade and the Welsh Office, and that we have complied meticulously with all the requirements of the Bank of England, I can only say I fully share your bewilderment,*" he said. "*We all earnestly believe that it is in the best public interest for full banking recognition to be given to our only Welsh bank, which has been the means of keeping thousands of people in profitable employment. Would it not be tragic to stifle this dedication and activity at such a sensitive time in our economic affairs?*

"*We can still carry on the business of banking, but it is going to be very much more difficult to continue to build upon the foundations we have so painstakingly established over the past eight years. And we will be at a considerable handicap in overseas trade unless we are a recognised bank, and seen to be so by our European and other contemporaries,*" added Sir Julian.

A shareholder asked what the First National Bank of Chicago, being the biggest shareholder in the Commercial Bank of Wales (outside the 29.6% total stake of the Hodge family), thought of this situation. The Chicago bank's director, George C. Bergland, said: "*We are, of course, very disappointed with the decision. We don't understand the reasons for it, but we fully support the board's efforts and believe the decision will be reversed.*"

Asked about rumours of a possible takeover, Sir Julian said: "*With your help we will win our appeal and get full banking recognition. When we get that we will get full listing on the Stock Exchange and increase our share capital to £10m. As a personal view I would expect to see our shares [£1] standing at perhaps 150p in the market.*"

The Commercial Bank of Wales managed to ride through that storm but its days were numbered. In 1986 the Bank of Scotland bought a 75% holding in the ailing company, for only 63.75p a share. With the take-over the Welsh enterprise was allowed to change its name to Bank of Wales (and its Welsh translation, Banc Cymru) under the chairmanship of former Secretary of State for Wales George Thomas, by then Lord Tonypandy.

In May 1991 the new chairman, Sir Alun Talfan Davies, said it was with an element of sadness that the board recommended acceptance of the Bank of Scotland's offer to increase its holding from 75% to 100%, at 70p a share – substantially higher than the 43p at which the Commercial Bank of Wales were then trading. At his Jersey home Sir Julian Hodge said the board had made the right decision, but he would have run the bank differently, and not got into this situation.

The final blow came on 25 September 2002, when the Bank of Scotland announced it was abolishing the name Bank of Wales, whose Cardiff headquarters had by then become the South Wales regional base of Bank of Scotland Business Banking. The Bank of Wales had never lived up to its ambitious national title, for its only branches were in Cardiff, Swansea, Newport and Carmarthen. The branch signs were changed to read Bank of Scotland during the autumn if 2002.

Chapter 8
Other banks of Wales

The 1986-2002 Bank of Wales was not the first to bear the impressive name. A Bank of Wales was established in May 1863, with an impressive capital of £500,000 in 5,000 shares. The Carmarthen bank of Waters, Jones & Co. failed in 1832, prompting the opening of a replacement by Biddulph Brothers & Co., who, in 1833 or 1834, also opened at Pembroke, which had been without a bank since the closure of the Waters, Jones branch.

John Biddulph, junior, of Llangennech, Carmarthenshire, and Francis Thomas Biddulph, of Crickmarren, Pembroke, were the second and third sons of John Biddulph of Ledbury. Their great uncle, Francis Biddulph, was the founder and senior partner of Biddulph, Cocks & Co., bankers at Charing Cross – who acted as London correspondents for the Carmarthen and Pembroke banks. The family had land at Llanelli where their name is perpetuated in Biddulph Street and the Biddulph Arms public house, in the town's New Street. John became a partner in the Charing Cross firm, while Francis Thomas Biddulph was the active partner in the Pembroke branch. In 1844 the Carmarthen bank ceased to exist, and the Pembroke bank opened a discount account with the Bank of England, thereupon ceasing to issue its own notes.

William Hulm, a clerk with Waters, Jones, had been retained by the Biddulph brothers at Carmarthen in 1832. By 1844 he was manager at Pembroke, and also agent for the County Fire & Provident Life Offices. By 1849 the Pembroke partners were Robert Somers Cocks, of Charing Cross, Robert Biddulph, of Charing Cross, and Francis Thomas Biddulph, of Crickmarren. In 1850 they sold the Pembroke bank to local grocer and attorney Robert Lock, and William Hulm, who was by then mayor of the borough. They continued to draw on what had become Cocks, Biddulph & Co. at Charing Cross, and in 1863 they opened a branch at Tenby.

On 30 June 1864 Lock and Hulm sold their enterprise to the Bank of Wales Ltd., which had been formed a year earlier. William Hulm remained manager at both Pembroke and Tenby. In that year the Bank of Wales had 170 shareholders, and held £27,445 in 463 deposit accounts, and £51,112 in 309 current accounts. It had branches, at Cardiff, Swansea, Newport, Neath, Pembroke, Pembroke Dock, Tenby, Usk, Bridgend, Briton ferry, Cowbridge, Haverfordwest and Hereford. During 1864 the Provincial Banking Corporation made a detailed study of the Bank of Wales, and agreed to amalgamate with it for the advantage to be gained from *"a large and profitable field of employment of capital at advantageous rates, which seems now to be the want of the Provincial Banking Corporation."*

In December 1864 the short-lived Bank of Wales amalgamated with the Provincial Banking Corporation and London & Provincial Bank Ltd., William Hulm again retaining his job as manager at Pembroke and Tenby. The Pembroke Dock branch was at first managed by James McLean who had earlier sold his small private bank to the Bank of Wales, but this, too, was soon placed under the management of Hulm, until his retirement at the end of 1876, aged 70.

London & Provincial Bank took over the bank of J. & W. Walters in 1872, with branches at Haverfordwest, Pembroke Dock and Narberth. The London & Provincial Bank was taken over by Barclays Bank in 1918.

London was always the hub of British banking, and Wales was the source of the best roast beef of old England, from its famous Welsh Black breed that was to feature on Richard Williams's money in 1969. Welsh beef was delivered on the hoof, in big herds, to pioneer today's basic road network between Wales and England. By the 18th century the same unsurfaced roads were being used to supply London with the even more famous Welsh mutton.

Drovers taking these animals across country, at a slow fourteen to sixteen miles a day, were the only men providing regular contact between Wales and London. As well as bringing back the proceeds of the sale of the livestock, they frequently conveyed large sums of money to London on behalf of Welsh landowners who had accounts to settle in the city. The ever-present risk of robbery on route, combined with the doubtful honesty of many of the drivers, led to the rationalisation of this two-way flow of gold, so that the animals themselves were used as walking cash, the actual gold remaining at either end. Thus a Welsh banking system was created.

What manner of men were the drovers? We know they were all married and over thirty years of age, and that they were householders. These were conditions laid down in the reigns of Edward VI and Elizabeth I for the granting of a drover's licence by the Justices of the Peace, assembled in Quarter Sessions. A drover caught without a licence was

Bronze Memorial to the Llandovery drovers

liable to be whipped and pilloried, under an all-embracing 16th century Act of Parliament designed to put an end to the *"many diseases and mischiefs which have happened before this time in the land of Wales, by the many wasters, rhymers, minstrels and other vagabonds"* – the legislation which led to the re-establishment of the National Eisteddfod of Wales in 1567, as a means of sorting out, by examination, the genuine poets and harpists from among the multitude of wandering beggars. Twm o'r Nant, the famous Denbighshire bard born in 1739, wished that *"all drovers deceiving the world had been hanged"*, judging from some of his poetry:

> *Llwyr wfft i borthmyn am dwyllo'r byd;*
> *O! na byddent I gyd on grogedig.*

He portrays them as cheats and drunkards, wandering from inn to inn with more concern for loose women to be found on route than for the welfare of the cattle entrusted to his care. George Borrow, journeying through North Wales nearly a century later, recorded the boast of an Anglesey drover that there was not a tavern between Pentraeth and Worcester at which he was not known. *"He was dressed in a pepper-and-salt coat of the Newmarket cut, breeches of corduroy, and brown top boots, and had on his head a broad, black, coarse, low-crowned hat. In his left hand he held a heavy whalebone whip with a brass head."*

On the other side of the coin we have the example of drovers being entrusted with the ship money collected in Denbighshire in 1636, for conveyance to the King's tax agent in London. In the following century one drover served Sir Watkin Williams Wynn, of Wynnstay, Ruabon, for forty years, and used to carry sums of gold as great as £400 to London. John Williams, Archbishop of York and Lord Keeper of the Great Seal, who garrisoned his native Conwy for King Charles during the Civil War, described the drovers as *"the Spanish fleet of North Wales which brings hither that little gold and silver we have"*. Benjamin Evans, a Pembrokeshire drover, became the pastor of a famous independent chapel at Llanuwchlyn in 1769. A Carmarthenshire drover, Dafydd Jones, of Caeo, became one of the foremost Welsh hymn-writers of the 18th century. He was the son of a drover, and a familiar figure as far afield as Maidstone fair. It was when returning home via Builth Wells that he was attracted by the sound of singing coming from Troedrhiwdalar chapel on a Sunday night. He went inside and was instantly converted.

Inn names, such as the Drovers Arms, to be found as far afield as Rhewl (near Ruthin), Mold, Knutsford and Ludlow, remind us of the routes used for this important trade. Cardigan Fair alone was said to be responsible for the export of 20,000 head of cattle a year, at the end of the 18th century. During that same period Anglesey was supplying 6,000 cattle a year, despite their first having to swim across the Menai Strait to commence the long walk to London. Between 1780 and

1850 the number of cattle sold at Smithfield rose from 100,000 to more than 250,000 per annum, and there was a growing market for as many beasts as Wales could supply.

Before setting out for their 250-300-mile journey the cattle had to be shod, each requiring eight shoes because of their cloven hoofs. The fee for making and fixing such a set at the beginning of the 19th century was 10 pence. There was nothing unusual in a shoe smith being suddenly presented with a herd of fifty to a hundred cattle, for quick shoeing, for which he had to throw each beast on to its side. Good throwers were highly respected members of the community at shoeing centres like Ffestiniog. They were, of course, men of great strength and regarded as being very brave, the matadors of Wales. They approached the beast from the front, grabbed a horn in each hand and proceeded to twist the animal's head until it fell to the ground, where it would be held until the shoes were in place.

One of the most famous of the Welsh shoe smiths was Huw Gruffydd of Dolwyddelan, who devised shoes for geese to enable them to waddle to London behind the cattle. The shoes were shaped like miniature iron stilts, which raised a goose's foot an inch or two above the ground. New replacement shoes were fitted at Aylesbury to enable the geese to complete the journey.

Having crossed the Menai Strait, the Anglesey drovers would proceed through the Nant Ffrancon Pass to Capel Curig, crossing the River Conwy at Llanrwst, and thence on to Abergele, Ruthin (for re-shoeing) and Llandegla, proceeding to England via either Llangollen or Wrexham. South Caernarvonshire drovers went via Llanystumdwy, Maentwrog, Bala and Llangollen. Merioneth drivers also went via Bala. Those of Denbighshire and Flintshire converged on Ruthin and Llandegla. Montgomeryshire drovers went via Bishop's Castle. North Pembrokeshire, Carmarthenshire and South Cardiganshire routes all converged on Llanymddyfri (Llandovery), where by 1799 farmer and innkeeper David Jones had established his Bank of the Black Ox. From Llanymddyfri the drovers proceeded into Breconshire via Pen-y-gefnffordd, where they were joined by the large herds from Tregaron. The South Wales farmers generally relied upon the Bristol market, to which they had easy access.

For his labours a late 18th century drover would be paid three shillings a day. That might look like exceptionally good money, being exactly the same as what was paid two centuries later to soldiers of the British Army during World War Two, but the drover had to hire his own assistants and pay for his keep during the journey. Drovers also got a bonus of

Bank of the Black Ox, now Lloyds TSB.

six shillings at the end of the journey, and were allowed to keep substantial money they could make by selling milk on route.

The universal drover's cry was "Haiptrw Ho!" shouted to warn farmers to keep their cattle out of the way, for there was little hope of recovering a beast that got mixed up with a large herd on the move. Neither could a drover be sure of recovering his herd if it stampeded, so that one of his greatest problems was keeping the animals calm for two or three weeks. When there was a reasonably good 19th century turnpike road the drover's task could, paradoxically, be made much more difficult, as is shown in a story preserved of one Wil Elis, of Trawsfynydd. Knowing a stagecoach was due from the opposite direction, Elis rode ahead of the herd to warn the coachman. Ignoring the drover's signals, perhaps believing Elis to be a highwayman, the coach driver whipped his horses into greater speed as he charged forward. Leaving his assistants to round up the frightened cattle, Wil Elis took advantage of a loop in the road to intercept the coach and, with a flick of his staff, overturn it, spilling driver, passengers and horses into the grass.

A drover's best friend and assistant was his dog. A Llandrillo-yn-Edeirnion drover named Clough, having arrived at a Kent fair, was persuaded to sell his horse for a good price. That left him with the choice of walking all the way home or taking a coach and leaving his faithful dog Carlo to fend for itself. He chose the latter course and attached part of his horse harness to the dog, together with a note requesting innkeepers to give it some food and send it on its way. Knowing all his master's favourite inns, Carlo called at each, was treated kindly, and returned to his Merioneth home within a week.

Instead of being entrusted with bags of gold and silver to transport between London and Wales it became a lot simpler to give the drovers pieces of paper, in the form of bills of exchange or promissory notes – initially for conversion into gold on demand. The Bank of England was established in 1694 by a group of London goldsmiths, in order to find a loan of £1,200,000 for King William III. The bank was allowed to issue promissory notes to the extent of its loan to the king. An Act of 1708 forbade the issue of notes by any new bank with more than six partners, thus giving the Bank of England a monopoly in joint stock banking.

It was in this situation that the small private banks of Wales emerged. Late 18th century industries such as the glove makers and shoemakers of Denbigh, who traded with London, banked their takings in the city and settled their debts by bills of exchange. However London was so remote that people in rural Wales found it easier to keep circulating bills of exchange as money, in lieu of the more familiar gold, silver and copper. That created a need for local banks associated with London agents.

There is a tradition that Banc y Llong (Bank of the Ship) was established at Aberystwyth harbour as early as 1762, when the Custom House was moved from Aberdyfi, although nothing is known about it until 1806, when it passed into the hands of John Jones, of Cardiganshire and London, and Thomas Morgan and David Jones, both of Aberystwyth. On the death of Morgan in 1808 Thomas Williams, of Aberystwyth, was admitted. The partnership was dissolved in 1815, after which Thomas Williams continued banking under the title of Williams, Davies & Co. Later Rice Jones, who had been apprenticed to the bank on its reorganisation in 1806, became a partner, in conjunction with Henry Benson, a local wine merchant, in what came to be known as Benson & Jones.

The North Wales Bank, later known as Flintshire Bank, was established at Holywell in about 1790, to become famous among coin collectors for its issue of silver and copper tokens during the currency famine of 1811. One side of the tokens showed crossed keys on a shield, surmounted by the Prince of Wales's feathers, and the legend "Flintshire Bank – August 12, 1811". The other side was inscribed "Flintshire Bank Token" and the value, e.g. "One shilling", together with the initials JOS&O for the partners Jones, Oldfield, Sankey and Oakley. The principal partner was Richard Sankey who also controlled a bank at Denbigh by 1817. Today's Bank Place, in Holywell, preserves the name of Bank Court named during Sankey's time.

In 1792 the Chester & North Wales Bank was launched with some of the wealth derived from the vast copper deposits of Amlwch. The founder was Owen Williams, son of Thomas Williams who, in 1778, formed the Parys Mine Company in partnership with the Reverend Edward Hughes, curate of Lleiniog, and John Dawes, a London banker. Owen Williams was later joined in his banking venture by Colonel William Hughes (later Lord Dinorben), of Kinmel, son of the Reverend Edward Hughes. By 1812 they had opened a branch at Caernarfon, where there was already a bank founded by Richard Roberts, agent to the Coed Helen Estate. Bangor branch was opened in 1822, followed by several others, including Amlwch and Llanfairfechan.

After the death of Richard Roberts, in January 1799, his bank was carried on by his brother Robert (died December 1809) and his son Richard (died 1828). Among the many letters received by Richard Williams in 1969 was one from Michael Roberts, of Farm Close, Wheatley, Oxford, saying he was a direct descendant of Richard Roberts, and giving 1775 as the date when the first Caernarfon bank was founded. He noted that it was later bought up by the Chester & North Wales Bank, and this in turn by Lloyds Bank.

In somewhat similar fashion to the Amlwch copper wealth behind the Chester and North Wales Bank, the copper of the Great Orme mines, at Llandudno, was used to inject capital into the firm of Douglas & Smalley, who opened banks at Holywell and Mold in the 1820s. John Douglas had a stake in the Tŷ Gwyn Mining Company, named after an old farm which stood near the entrance to the present Llandudno pier. Christopher Smalley died in 1829 and Douglas died in October 1839, after which many people lost their savings when the bank went bankrupt. Both were involved in the Holywell cotton industry.

A grocer named James Kenrick began banking as a sideline at his Wrexham shop in 1800. Later he abandoned the groceries and flourished as a banker until the disastrous run on the banks in 1847. Failure of country banks was commonplace between 1793 and 1825. The landing of American-led French troops in Pembrokeshire in 1797, with the aim of marching on Chester and Liverpool, caused panic and a run on the Bank of England, whose gold reserves became so depleted that the Government authorised the suspension of payment on its bank notes. For more than twenty years Bank of England notes could not be converted, so that the value of a £5 note fell to £3-11s in relation to the private notes of solid country banks. In that situation the slightest local rumour could ruin the local bank. The Government did little to encourage confidence: in 1810 the Receiver General of Taxes in Wales gave notice that he would not accept local notes. That prompted a matching lack of faith and similar refusal to accept local notes by the traders of towns like Caernarfon.

After 1808 it was necessary to obtain a licence to issue notes, but there was no regulation as to the quantity that could be circulated. Anyone prepared to pay the annual licence fee of £30, and the stamp duty on each note, could print as many as he could induce the public to take, but the denomination could not be less than £1. Cash reserves held by country banks against their notes and other liabilities were usually very small, but most of them maintained accounts with one of the London private banks. The London agent collected bills of exchange and made payments. Drafts and post bills ("after sight" bills) and letters of credit were drawn on the London bank. It also became a growing practice to make country bank notes payable in London as well as at source.

Forgeries were commonplace. So were close imitations of reputable notes, as instanced in 1823 when John Dicas brought an action against the *Manchester Guardian* for calling him "*a prison bird and confessed pauper*". The *Guardian* lost the case, but not before they had proved that after serving a two-year prison sentence for bankruptcy offences Dicas induced some Holywell businessmen to join him in founding the Flintshire New Bank, which issued notes closely resembling those of the original Flintshire Bank. It was a hollow victory, for the publicity resulted in the collapse of Mr. Dicas's bank.

If the slightest whisper could close a bank, a nonchalant display of confidence could have the opposite effect. In December 1825 the *North Wales Gazette* declared: "*We feel happy in being able to congratulate our readers that not the slightest rumour or doubt has attached to the stability and credit of all the banks connected with the Principality.*" However in the spring of 1826 Williams & Co. – the name by which the Chester & North Wales Bank had come to be recognised – announced that their Caernarfon branch would not accept the notes of other local banks except at a discount of 5%.

So as to ensure a healthy flow of gold throughout the country, the Bank Notes Act, 1826, prohibited the issue, in England, of notes for less than £5. The same legislation also prohibited existing private banks from making new issues of notes for less than £5 after 1828, resulting in a protest meeting in Mold. By 1832 Richard Myddleton Lloyd, of Wrexham, was the only North Wales banker still issuing his own notes.

Under the new legislation the Bank of Manchester was formed in 1828, and opened a branch at Newtown, but it was wound up in 1842. Another Manchester enterprise, the Northern & Central Bank of England, was launched in 1833, soon to open forty branches, including Caernarfon, Bangor, Denbigh, Holywell, Mold and Wrexham.

Bank of England notes were declared legal tender in 1833, from when no one could demand gold when offered a bank note in settlement of a debt. It also meant that country banks could redeem their own notes simply by exchanging them for Bank of England notes. By the same Act the notes of the Bank of England were deprived of their legal tender status in, of all places, a corner of the Bank of England. That was a counter specifically set aside as a redemption department where, ultimately, one could obtain gold. The 1833 Act permitted joint stock banks to carry on business in London provided they did not issue notes within the already prohibited 65-mile radius of the Bank of England. Other problems remained, such as the hostility of the Bank of England and existing London private banks which, until as late as 1854, refused to admit joint stock banks to the Clearing House.

The North & South Wales Bank, whose name can still be found carved into the stonework of what are now HSBC banks at Colwyn Bay and Holyhead, was founded at Liverpool in 1836. For at least two centuries the commerce of North Wales had been linked to the port of Liverpool – the principal store in countless

The name of the North and South Wales Bank lives on within the HSBC at Colwyn Bay. The heraldry over the front door links Liverpool's maritime wealth to the Dragon of Wales.

small towns proudly carrying the name Liverpool House, to indicate the impeccable source of its best goods. For the same reason the principal stores of countless South Wales towns were called Bristol House – the historical insignificance of Cardiff, destined to become the capital of Wales in 1955, can be gauged by the fact that it did not have a bank until 1792.

With an authorised share capital of £600,000, the North & South Wales Bank opened in Cook Street, Liverpool, in April, pending the building of new headquarters in James Street. They had secured a licence to print their own notes, under the 1826 Act, and twenty-two North and South Wales towns were named as issuing centres although no branches yet existed outside Liverpool. The directors invested in a phaeton and "a strong horse", and appointed a high-powered team to travel into Wales with wide powers to buy up existing banks, appoint staff, open new banks, buy suitable property, and sell shares to anyone who asked for them. Richard Sankey, of Holywell and Denbigh, was one of the first to sell out, for a pension of £500 a year to himself or his wife if she survived him. He also bought shares in the new enterprise. Benson & Jones, of Aberystwyth, followed suit, selling their premises for £3,000.

An unexpected crisis arose soon afterwards, involving the convening of a special meeting of shareholders at Liverpool, to decide whether or not the head office should operate as a bank. It was argued that Welshmen might get the impression their deposits were intended to advance the business of the Port of Liverpool, and *"this company would therefore have no greater claim to the title of a Welsh National Bank than any other joint stock company which might choose to establish branches in the Principality"*. The intention of the founders was thus quite clear: their registered title of North & South Wales Bank really meant the Welsh National Bank, or Bank of Wales. However, the meeting got around that problem by arguing that Liverpool was the commercial metropolis of North Wales, and that it was essential for head office to be in the city, and to conduct business in the economic centre.

The meeting attracted the attentions of the *News & Sunday Herald* which, in its issue of 12 June, 1836, said of the North & South Wales Bank: *"The directors are composed of persons of different religious as well as political feelings. And though we cannot do otherwise than deprecate the admission of Tories into any association at all, we can tolerate them when they behave decently and lose the rancorous spirit which so frequently distinguishes the clique."*

In January 1837 a deputation of directors of the North & South Wales Bank was in Cardiff and Brecon, negotiating to buy private banks in those towns, when they received letters instructing them to break off negotiations and return to Liverpool. That was the nearest the North & South Wales Bank ever got to South Wales, and it never became the intended National Bank of Wales – their southernmost branch was opened in 1904 at Carmarthen. On their return to Liverpool the directors discovered that news had reached the managers of the impending collapse of the

Manchester-based Northern & Central Bank of England, with its eight North Wales branches, and with a note issue of nearly £400,000 in circulation. The North & South Wales Bank took over all the North Wales branches of their rival (which went into liquidation in 1839), to create what some saw as an alarming situation. One may judge the state of Welsh banks at that time by the evidence given to a House of Commons Select Committee on Joint Stock Banks, in 1838. A Mr.Turner, agent of the Liverpool branch of the Bank of England, deposed:

"The competence and respectability of the people of the branches, I should say, must be very low indeed. In travelling through Wales two years ago I could not help seeing that they were carrying on banking almost farcically, for instead of meeting one's ideas of a respectable establishment, there was a small cottage, more like a huckster's shop than a bank, with BANK written in great characters over it."

The result of this acquisition was to give the North & South Wales Bank a paid up capital of £159,000 and deposits of £140,000, against loans and a note issue of £367,000. A financial crisis was sweeping the country so that by the end of 1839 the bank had to borrow £110,000 from the London & Westminster Bank (founded in 1834), at the same time pledging all their securities and undertaking to liquidate their Liverpool business except that which was essential for their North Wales branches.

By good management, and as a purely temporary measure, they managed to reduce their note issue over the next four years, during which time no dividend was paid to shareholders. This was the situation when the Bank Charter Act was passed in 1844, with the long-term aim of concentrating all note-issuing activities on the Bank if England, for greater security in redemption. Existing country banks were allowed to continue issuing notes, over £5 in value, but only up to the average amount in circulation during the twelve weeks ending 27 April 1844. The privilege would lapse if the bank amalgamated with any other bank, or opened an office in London, or suspended its note issue. The effect of this on the North & South Wales Bank was to limit their note issue to £63,951, a very small sum in relation to their future operations.

The affairs of the North & South Wales Bank were at a very low ebb when George Rae, a 28-years-old Scotsman, was appointed general manager in 1845. After training with the North of Scotland Bank he had joined the Liverpool staff in April 1839 as inspector of branches. His contribution to the story of Welsh banking was monumental, for it was he who had to steer the company, and the hopes of thousands of customers, through the financial storm of 1847.

On 22 October 1847 *The Express,* a London newspaper specialising in business news, announced that the North & South Wales Bank had stopped payment. The report was untrue but there were no telephones in those days, and by the time it was corrected it was too late. Within two days the bank had to suspend business, a victim of a national money crisis rather than its own instability. As George Rae told the *Liverpool Mercury* on 29 October: *"The report exploded amongst our branches like a shell, and literally blew the bank up. Traversing a large aggregate of liabilities in a few hours, and at twenty different points, without notice, without an instant of time allowed us to turn in, it rolled back upon the Head Office a volume of demands impossible to meet."*

The North & South Wales Bank had only just recovered from an internal crisis that began in 1844 when it took over Cefn Colliery, near Ruabon, following the inability of the owners to repay an overdraft of £20,000. The bank found itself involved in an old feud between the workers of Cefn and the nearby rival Plas Kyneston mine. At Ruthin Assizes, in March 1843, eight men employed by Pickering & Co., at Cefn, were charged with maliciously filling in a shaft at the Plas Kynaston mine of T.E. Ward. The men were convicted and released at the request of Mr. Ward and on giving an undertaking not to repeat the offences. However, at the summer assizes fifteen men employed by Ward were charged with maliciously flooding Cefn Colliery by building a dam and diverting a river. The case dragged on into 1844, by which time the bank was the owner of Cefn and regarded as the real prosecutor. It ended with an agreement not to proceed with the indictment.

While losing money rapidly at Cefn Colliery the North & South Wales Bank was also faced with the embarrassment of financing the conversion of Wallasey Pool into the Port of Birkenhead. Anxious to share in the shipping wealth of Liverpool, on the opposite shore of the Mersey, the citizens of Birkenhead began the costly project of damming the mouth of the pool and constructing a low water basin and docks. The foundation stone was laid on 23 October 1844, from which date the dock commissioners made ever-increasing demands on the bank. Work came to an abrupt end in October 1847, after the run on the bank. Morpeth and Egerton Docks had been officially opened on 5 April 1847, but the low water basin, which was the most important part of the plan, was far from complete, and only a temporary embankment stood where the dam was supposed to be built across Wallasey Pool. The scheme did not restart until 1858 when Birkenhead Dock Estate was transferred to the Mersey Docks & Harbour Board.

That was the background to the problems faced by George Rae at the start of the 1847 money crisis. He went to Liverpool and Birmingham in search of

The Prince of Wales feathers and other details from the Wales Bank's branch at Charing Cross, Birkenhead. The 'feathers' emblem can still be seen at many of Midland's branches in North Wales, the Wirral and Liverpool.

funds, and tried to persuade the Scottish banks to re-discount bills that were being refused in London. During the middle of October both the Royal Bank of Liverpool and the Liverpool Banking Company collapsed, causing another panic run on the Liverpool branch of the North & South Wales Bank. The Bank of England refused to help, and the North & South Wales Bank resorted to creating additional capital of £100,000 in 7% preference shares. Depositors were persuaded to accept post-dated bills to mature in six instalments over eighteen months for the sum deposited. North Wales endorsement of the plan was crucial to its success, and the bank arranged a series of public meetings across the region.

As a further step to recovery the North & South Wales Bank closed their Bangor and Dolgellau branches, and sold their Cardigan branch to a private bank. Their Porthmadog, Pwllheli and Ffestiniog branches were sold to John Casson, brother of a Blaenau Ffestiniog slate quarry owner, who founded the new banking company of Cassons & Co. At Pwllheli Hugh Pugh, who had been a cashier with the North & South Wales Bank, set up his own rival bank, taking with him many of Casson's intended customers.

Closure of the Bangor branch caused a run on the nearby bank of Williams & Co., who had planned for just such an eventuality. Staff turned up to find a rapidly growing crowd of customers clamouring for their money. The doors were opened to reveal barrels of shiny gold sovereigns behind the counter. Everyone was paid in full, without question, and confidence was soon restored, and the crowd dispersed, but only just in time. Only the staff knew that there was but a thin layer of sovereigns on top of a pile of sawdust. A similar ruse was used at the Welshpool branch of Beck's Bank – Messrs Beck, Dodson, Beck & Eaton – in that same year of 1847. A mob had gathered outside when the Earl of Powis came to the rescue, appearing in person ostensibly to deposit his collected rents. His staff laid down his bags of gold, the tops all open to reveal the contents, and the Earl rounded on the crowd for their silly behaviour. They melted away, not knowing there was only a thin layer of coins on the top of bags of chaff. Both Williams & Co. and Becks eventually merged with Lloyds.

Lloyds Bank preserves the name of Samuel Lloyd, a Quaker, of Dolobran, Meifod, in Montgomeryshire. He was born in a Welsh prison while his parents were incarcerated because of their refusal to swear allegiance to King Charles II. He became involved in iron smelting in Montgomeryshire and Denbighshire, and in 1698 moved to Birmingham. There he expanded his smelting into the manufacture of nails. His son, also named Sampson, became a prosperous iron merchant and in 1765, at 66 years of age, he decided to venture into banking, in partnership with button-maker John Taylor. They founded Birmingham's first bank, Taylors & Lloyds, with a capital of £6,000 in only four shares. After the death of Taylor's son, in 1852, the bank became Lloyds & Co., becoming a joint stock bank in 1865.

The North & South Wales Bank resumed normal business at the end of January 1848, albeit with a much smaller empire. In 1856 they bought the Knighton branch of the Kington & Radnorshire Bank, whose owners had put it on the market because of widespread confusion between the names Knighton and Kington. In the same year North & South Wales Bank launched a savings scheme for the dockers of Birkenhead, later extending the plan to Rhyl. In 1863 they opened three new branches within the city of Liverpool. Ten years later they moved their head office to 60-62 Castle Street.

A noticeable lack of North & South Wales Bank expansion in the North Wales towns they had briefly dominated, in their bid to create a Welsh national bank, was due to an informal agreement with the National Provincial Bank of England on spheres of influence. Founded at Gloucester in 1833, the National Provincial Bank of England had taken an early interest in Wales, and got close to becoming a national bank for Wales, despite its Anglophile name. Brecon was the location for its second branch,

The seal of the original National Provincial Bank of England at Colwyn Bay can still be read in the stonework of the old Pwllycrochan estate office in Station Road.

opened in 1834. Within three years it had branches at Aberystwyth, Amlwch, Cardiff, Dolgellau, Newcastle Emlyn, and Pwllheli, with sub-branches at Bridgend, Bont-faen, Bala, Machynlleth, Tremadog, and Porthmadog. In 1868 it acquired the business of Crawshay, Bailey & Co., with branches at Newport, Monmouth and Abergavenny. It also acquired the Carmarthen business of David Morris & Sons (founded c.1791, using a cockerel as his symbol on his note issues). Other Welsh branches followed. In 1918 it briefly became the National Provincial and Union Bank of England Ltd., and the following year absorbed the Llangollen Old Bank, founded in 1854 by Charles & Watkin Richards. It eventually dropped the "of England" bit in 1924, when it became the National Provincial Bank Ltd. In 1962 The National Provincial Bank absorbed District Bank Ltd., which was the new name adopted in 1924 for the Manchester & Liverpool District Banking Company, which opened its first Welsh branch at Colwyn Bay in 1908. The N.P. bank, as it was popularly known, merged with Westminster Bank Ltd. in 1969, to form the National Westminster Bank, which merged with the Royal Bank of Scotland in 2002, but retains its name as NatWest.

The post-1860 agreement on zones of influence between the North & South Wales Bank and the National Provincial Bank of England lasted until 1908, with each bank advising the other of any changes in rate, and undertaking to adhere to

HSBC Holyhead still preserves the name of the North and South Wales Bank.

the rate quoted. After the early 1860s all new branches of the North & South Wales Bank were recorded as being opened "by arrangement with the N.P.Bank." In 1856 there was a well-known quarrel between the rival Holyhead branch managers, one accusing the other of having "seduced a customer" by offering him $4\frac{1}{2}\%$ on deposits. Today those Holyhead branches still carry their original names carved into the stonework.

In 1873 the North & South Wales Bank bought the Dolgellau and Barmouth operations of Williams & Sons, usually known as Old Merionethshire Bank. This bank was founded before 1803 by Thomas & Hugh Jones. Lewis Williams married a granddaughter of Thomas Jones and became the sole proprietor, later taking in his sons. Residents of Dolgellau and Barmouth preferred their notes to those of the Bank of England, and in 1844 their authorised note issue was £11,000. In 1875 North & South Wales Bank paid £12,000 to buy out Cassons & Co., who had added Blaenau Ffestiniog and Harlech to their original three branches. At the end of December 1876 North & South Wales Bank took over the Bala, Corwen and Dolgellau branches of the Bala Banking Co.,

The name of The National Provincial Bank of England can still be read over the door of today's NatWest Bank at Holyhead.

founded in 1864 with a capital of £9,000, and which had just closed its doors because of the failure of a Liverpool corn merchant.

The North & South Wales Bank was fighting back, still with the original declared aim of becoming the national Bank of Wales. In 1879 that claim was formally challenged and demolished by the formation of a company with the registered title of National Bank of Wales Ltd. Its head office was in Manchester but was moved to Aberdare the following year. In 1882 control passed to a group of Cardiff businessmen and the head office was moved yet again, to the future capital of Wales. At first concentrating on South Wales industrial business, the new

THE LONDON CITY & MIDLAND BANK LIMITED.

NORTH AND SOUTH WALES BANK BRANCH,

62, CASTLE STREET,

Please quote No. *2369*
in all correspondence.

LIVERPOOL.

16 Dec 1908.

DEAR SIR (or MADAM),

NORTH AND SOUTH WALES BANK

AMALGAMATION.

We beg to acknowledge the receipt from you

to-day of Certificate representing _____*37*_____ Shares in

the NORTH AND SOUTH WALES BANK, LIMITED.

Yours faithfully,

T. ROWLAND HUGHES,

Liverpool Manager.

Robt. Roberts Esq.

National Bank of Wales pushed north in 1890, acquiring the chain of branches formed by Hugh Pugh, of Pwllheli, during the 1847 troubles of the North & South Wales Bank. Alas, it turned out to be both a reckless and fraudulent move, ending in imprisonment for some of the directors. No allowance had been made for bad debts totalling a massive £80,000 on the books of Pugh's Bank. Furthermore, a sum of £30,000 was alleged to have been misappropriated during the negotiations, for sharing secretly between the general manager and two directors of the National Bank of Wales.

In 1893 the Metropolitan & Birmingham Bank (founded in 1829) agreed to take over the National Bank of Wales, paying not less than £110,000 for goodwill. That was but the start of a chain of disputes between the Metropolitan Bank and the liquidator, resulting in litigation, which revealed that for some years the august-sounding National Bank of Wales had been paying dividends out of capital. Unsecured loans had been made to the general manager and some of the directors, and balance sheets were false. It was calculated that the Metropolitan lost £500,000 on the deal. They took it in their stride and by the end of the year had 67 Welsh branches, including two in the north, at Llandudno and Llangefni, when they changed their name to Metropolitan Bank of England & Wales. They amalgamated with Midland Bank in 1914. (Midland Bank was founded at Birmingham in 1836.)

The North & South Wales Bank plodded on, occasionally reviving the idea of spreading into South Wales to justify their title, but never doing much about it. They had survived, without difficulty, the financial crises of 1857 and 1866, but a much greater problem was the dollar crisis of 1907, because the core of their business was in the Port of Liverpool, which was closely linked to the American market. The directors initiated negotiations for a merger with the Midland Bank, who were without a branch in North Wales. The agreement became effective at the end of 1908, when the last Welsh bank notes were withdrawn from circulation, under the provisions relating to mergers in the Bank Charter Act, 1844. The total value of North & South Wales Bank notes in circulation at the time of the merger was £37,000. The terms for the 1908 merger were seven Midland shares (of £60 with £12-10s paid up) and £3-10s cash for ten North & South Wales Bank shares (of £40 with £10 paid up). Four directors of the North & South Wales Bank were elected to the Board of Midland Bank. In 1992 Midland Bank was bought by the Hongkong & Shanghai Banking Corporation (which was founded at Hong Kong in 1865), resulting in its change of name to HSBC in September 1999, when all references to "Midland" were removed from its buildings.

Llandudno shopkeeper Derek Ellis offers a fistfull of cardboard change for a purchase with one of Richard Williams's Welsh pound notes.

It will be recalled that ever since October 1968 Richard Williams had been sending monthly invoices, totalling £1,200,000 a time, to the twenty-five British banks he said owed him money for using the universal numeric cheque encoding system he claimed to have invented. His calculations were based on a penny royalty for every cheque used.

In 1975 he decided to take a test case to court, and chose the Swansea branch of Lloyds Bank for a nominal claim for "a sum of not more than £1,000 in respect of copyright". He also sought an injunction to prevent Lloyds from using his encoding system without payment of royalties. Lloyds responded by asking Swansea County Court to strike out the case on the grounds that it disclosed no reasonable cause of action and/or was frivolous and vexatious and/or was an abuse of the process of the court.

Williams represented himself, and after three hours of legal argument with the impressive Lloyds Bank legal team the Court Registrar ruled that Mr. Williams's case should be allowed to proceed, and be transferred to the Chancery Division. He awarded Williams costs against the bank.

In support of his claim Williams said that in 1955 he wrote and published a book entitled *The Electronic Office* in which he set out the encoding system later adopted by all the banks. At that time Williams was working as a clerk for Midland Bank. As a result of his book, and the ideas he had outlined, he was appointed London general manager of the American-owned company Remington Rand Univac, in the middle of 1956. It was for Remington Rand that he demonstrated his system at an international exhibition in Frankfurt in April 1958. He had not sought a patent for his system, explaining: *"A patent lasts for only seventeen years, but I claim the copyright in the system, and I have evidence to prove it."*

Williams's long fight with the banks had been costly. In 1970 Robert Maxwell's Pergamon Press took his pioneering company Computer Consultants Ltd. to court, to obtain a winding up order so as to recover money owing for printing and distributing books written by Williams and his daughter Carys. When he appeared before Bangor Bankruptcy Court he told the official receiver that Computer Consultants Ltd. was owed £48m by the banks. With the demise of Computer Consultants Ltd. he made alternative arrangements for another of his enterprises, Williams Cheque Clearing Company, to resume invoicing the banks, which by 1975 owed him over £500m, he asserted.

Lloyds said the encoding system was devised in the United States and given to them, and other banks, free of charge, by the American Bankers' Association. *"I had demonstrated my system to European bankers long before the Americans got their hands on it,"* responded Williams.

It was Monday 28 February 1977 before the case reached the High Court, before Sir Robert Megarry, the Vice-Chancellor. Still arguing his own case, Williams said any damages awarded would be given to his company for distribution to the shareholders. He contended that the banks had infringed the copyright in his drawings relating to the position of a machine-readable strip on cheques, enabling them to be computer sorted. As a result he had lost royalties on his design.

The bank did not admit that Mr. Williams or his company owned the copyright in the drawings on which the cheques were based. It denied that any drawings by him were copied or reproduced, or that he or his company had suffered the losses alleged.

Williams told the court he produced specimen cheques in the 1950s as examples that might be suitable for computer work, and he gave British bankers a demonstration of his proposed computerised banking system. In October 1976 his company invited subscriptions to a "risk issue" of 200,000 ordinary £1 shares to finance his court action. He had warned investors that they might not get their money back, but that if he were successful they stood to receive a possible return of 3,000 to 1.

"The amount we are claiming is high by any standards. It is estimated to be something of the order of £600-odd million. From the research that has gone into the preparation of this case it now seems we also have a title to the American rights in this thing, and we have had discussions with top American lawyers with a view to extending the claim to all the American banks," he told the judge.

The case lasted several days. When the court convened on Monday 7 March, for the sixth day of the hearing, Richard Williams handed an affidavit to Vice-Chancellor Megarry saying he could not continue with his case because the judge had, the previous Friday, discharged a *subpoena* requiring witnesses from the accountants Price Waterhouse & Co. to give evidence.

Sir Robert said that although Mr. Williams was not continuing with his case Lloyds Bank were entitled to go ahead with their counter claim for a declaration that they had not infringed any copyright of Mr. Williams.

For the bank, Brian Dillon, QC, said Lloyds Bank cheque clearing system was derived from the American Bankers' Association system, after research and modification. There was no shred of evidence to show it was based on anything claimed by Mr. Williams. To succeed Mr. Williams would have to show there was a chain of copying from his system of magnetic ink strips for automatic cheque sorting.

The hearing lasted until Friday 18 March, when the judge told Williams that on the evidence before him the claim that any of his ideas had been used by the bank had not been proved. In a friendly word to Mr. Williams, Sir Robert praised the way in which he had presented his case with politeness and courtesy. Referring to

Williams's statement that he would fight on, after discontinuing his own case a week earlier, the judge said: *"Of course he is entitled to pursue any legitimate claim which he considers he has against anyone, but I hope he will consider very carefully any future litigation based on the materials he put before me."*

"In my judgement," said Sir Robert, *"not only is there no evidence that the bank directly or indirectly copied his drawings, but there is a substantial body of evidence to support the proposition that they could not have done so."* He noted that Mr. Williams, who had at one time worked in a bank, had for a long time been enthusiastic for the application of scientific methods, writing books and lecturing on the matter, adding: *"I think he came on the scene at a relatively early date. However others were there before him."* Costs were awarded against the plaintiff company, Williams' Cheque Clearing Company Ltd., owned by Mr. and Mrs. Williams.

Outside the court Williams said: *"I was deprived of the evidence I required from Price Waterhouse, and could not continue my case."* He said he intended appealing against the Vice-Chancellor's ruling.

On 31 July 1977 Richard Williams put his private affairs in the hands of the Official Receiver. He said his only debt was a Lloyds Bank claim for £532 and he had gone to the Receiver in order to rid himself of the bank's attentions over an alleged debt he did not regard as owing, and which he had no intention of paying. It arose out of his attempt to have "any other business" added to the agenda for the bank's annual general meeting, on 31 March, which he was entitled to attend as a shareholder – holding just a single share. On the day before the AGM a High Court judge found in favour of Lloyds Bank, who had objected to Williams's declared intention to distribute to the shareholders a letter, which the bank said was confidential, having been disclosed to Williams only for the purpose of his unsuccessful court case earlier in the month. *"The £532 is paltry in relation to the £600,000,000 the banks, including Lloyds, owe me,"* he said.

"I no longer have shares in the Black Sheep Company, successor to the Chief Treasury of Wales, who issued my Welsh money. The company carries on, and will honour its notes, although bank note collectors are unlikely to sell back something worth far more than the face value," said Williams.

By the time Williams eventually appeared before Bangor Bankruptcy Court, on 25 January 1978, he admitted the Statement of his affairs, showing gross liabilities of £99,168, but said that after taking account of his assets of £25, 227,260 he had a surplus of £25,184,280. He said more than £34,000 of his liabilities were debts to his own family and companies with which he was associated, including a loan and interest amounting to £20,000 he had to repay his wife, and £3,000 due to her for company management fees. Other alleged debts to solicitors, plant hire companies, and a firm of estate agents were disputed by him. Claims by banks should, he said, be offset against claims made by him against them. He admitted owing £3,591 to his note-issuing Black Sheep Company of Wales, but said he was owed £10,000 by Williams' Cheque Clearing Company (i.e. himself) for services rendered and expenses incurred in pursuing his unsuccessful 1977 case against Lloyds Bank.

Asked by Registrar William Jones whether the anticipated £25m surplus was a good debt, Williams replied: *"I say very good, unless you have any doubt about the solvency of the banks."* He said he had withdrawn his appeal against the way in which his 1977 case against Lloyds Bank had been handled, so that he could pursue his claims against the American banks.

"I am going to the United States in a few weeks, to brief experts to get on with my claim against 12,000 different banking companies," he said, adding that the American banks owed him about £5,000,000,000 for using his cheque encoding system.

Closing the examination, the Registrar said because of its complications the case did not, at first sight, appear to be a proper one in which to make the usual order granting automatic discharge from bankruptcy after five years.

On 20 December 1982 two High Court judges, Lord Justice May and Mr. Justice Comyn, sitting in the Queen's Bench Division, made an order prohibiting Williams from launching any more litigation without the court's special permission. The order was made at the request of the Solicitor-General, Sir Ian Percival, QC, who reviewed a ten-year history of Williams's court actions. Williams responded by challenging Lord Justice May's right to hear the case in view of the fact that he had also sat at another case, brought by Williams, two months earlier.

Announcing the order, Lord Justice May said Mr. Williams had launched vexatious legal proceedings and had used them to oppress his opponents. He had made himself bankrupt in the process. *"Mr. Williams has convinced himself that he has the right to claim against the clearing banks tens of millions of pounds for alleged breaches of what he considers to be his copyright in the computerised process for placing numbers at the bottom of cheques.*

"He has started several actions over his claim, plus others in what he considered to be a campaign to obtain more democratic representation on the boards of banks. A third group of actions arose after the Gas Corporation laid pipes across his land. Mr. Williams claimed the work caused damage and pollution to lakes on his land and the fish in them. The various claims were frivolous, vexatious and an abuse of the process of the courts," added Lord Justice May.

Outside the court Williams said: *"Pompous use of the courts by the Solicitor-General shows that the ordinary little man does not have a hope of finding justice."* Far from being silenced he would now be appealing against the way in which his claim against Lloyds Bank ended in 1977, after the judge refused him access to essential witnesses. He said ten years of lost cases had cost him £35,000 in legal fees. *"But I have enjoyed every penny of it, knowing I must win if the courts will only look at my documentary evidence going back to 1954,"* he added.

Ignoring the High Court ruling, Richard Williams petitioned the European

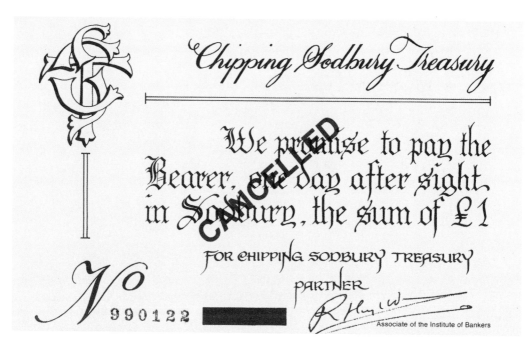

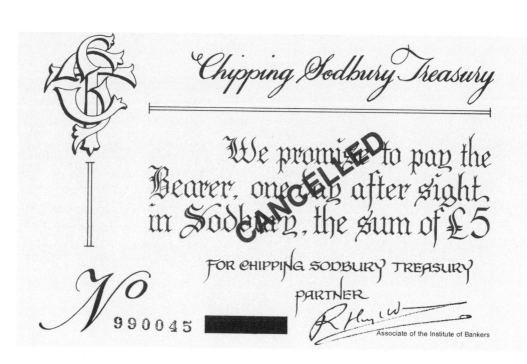

Council's Commission of Human Rights, backed by the United Nations, in 1984 to hear his claim against the British clearing banks. He supplied every bank with a copy of the registration of his claim, No, 11094/84, and the appointment of a Rapporteur to pursue the matter at Strasbourg, but he had been advised of a long delay in hearing human rights cases.

Meanwhile Richard Williams again turned his attention to note issuing. In June 1985 he issued two notes for £1 and £5, in the name of the Chipping Sodbury Treasury. The backs of the notes carried two specially painted street scenes of Chipping Sodbury, in Avon, painted by local artist Alan Roberts. The fronts were inscribed: *"We promise to pay the bearer one day after sight in Sodbury, the sum of £1. For Chipping Sodbury Treasury, partner R.Hugh Williams, Associate of the Institute of Bankers"* (with a matching inscription for the £5 note). They carried the black patch which had featured on his very first Welsh note in 1969. The Chipping Sodbury Treasury was actually Richard Williams's home, at Brynrhedyn Farm, a 24-acre holding including a trout breeding lake at Glan Conwy, to where he had moved from Llandudno.

"I rather liked the name of the place," he said, adding that his notes were designed to help the people of Chipping Sodbury who objected to the demise of the Bank of England's £1 note, following the introduction of the current £1 coin in 1983. *"They tried to print their own £1 notes in February, but they were illegal. I have come to their aid with the formula I used for my Welsh money in 1969, which was eventually endorsed by the Government as a perfectly legal issue. My Chipping Sodbury notes are equally legal, and of course they do not need the 2d tax stamp which the Government abolished to get me off their back,"* said Mr. Williams.

How were the good people of Chipping Sodbury to exchange their notes one day after sight, when their treasury was in the Conwy Valley asked the author. *"The issue of Sodbury's own cash will enable the people to exchange their £1 notes freely among themselves, instead of having to put up with the unpopular £1 coins. The village has four banks that are obliged, by their trade description literature, to collect any Chipping Sodbury Treasury notes, and present them to the Treasury for redemption,"* he explained.

Chapter 10

America's veto

In 1979 Williams told the American Bar Association that his unsuccessful action against Lloyds Bank left him with two options: to appeal in the British courts or "move the action to its root", in the USA. He supplied the Association with a file setting out his claim in the name of Computer Research Ltd., another of the £100 companies owned by himself and his wife. *"We claim all the rights to all types of magnetic cheque encoding,"* he declared.

His file included a copy of his 1955 book *The Electronic Office*, written while he was working as a clerk for Midland Bank, at Chester. On 9 May 1955 he had sent a copy to Burroughs Adding Machines Ltd., London, who replied in the 16th asking: *"Have you any objection to my submitting this to our technical people, even outside of Great Britain?"* With his book he had sent specimens of his proposed computer readable "cheques of the future" which he said he had been distributing at his lectures on the subject.

That, claimed Williams, was the start of the American system, which Lloyds had said, in court, was given to them over a free lunch in Miami, i.e. while denying they had copied Williams's system Lloyds had admitted using the American system. Also in Williams's file was a letter dated 9 February 1955 from Remington Rand, inviting him to an interview arising out of a paper he had submitted with the title of *Bank bookkeeping of the future*.

Williams's file outlined what he regarded as the history of the American development of cheque encoding for automated sorting. He said Stamford Research Institute was contracted by the Bank of America, in May 1951, to design a computer for a banking system. Stamford Research subsequently devised what was known as the ERMA system, using printed coded bars, which they suggested should go on the backs of cheques. The American Bankers' Association appointed a sub-committee to investigate cheque handling in April 1954, and in January 1955 the sub-committee emphasised the need for co-operation between the banks in cheque design. The ABA did not specify a design or supply an illustration. In May 1955 Stamford Research said the banks themselves would have to decide where to put the ERMA encoding – which General Electric Company of America took over. By that time, said Williams, the specimen cheques he had distributed while lecturing about his own invention were in wide circulation on both sides of the Atlantic.

On 10 May 1955, the day on which they would have received Williams's *The Electronic Office* at their London office, Burroughs invited the American Bankers' Association's cheque design sub-committee to meet them for discussions. In July

1956 the ABA adopted the concept of magnetic ink character recognition, which Williams said he had been lecturing about since 1954. By September 1957 Burroughs had a good working reader and encoder, which operated with fluorescent, not magnetic ink. Williams claimed the world's first effective computerised banking system was that which he demonstrated at Frankfurt in April 1958. As recently as 1959 the American National Association of Bank Auditors and Controllers proposed, to a meeting of Chicago bankers, an automated cheque sorting system that would have required every cheque to be photocopied onto cards, into which data could be punched by an operator for mechanical punched-card sorting – leaving the original cheques to pass through the banking system in the normal way, at a time when they were always returned to the drawer after they had been processed.

In February 1978 Williams's Computer Research Ltd. wrote to all the major printers of bank cheques saying the existing system of numeric encoding was open to fraud. He offered a better alternative. Two of the firms replied, saying it would be too expensive to make the suggested changes. The alternative offered by Williams was what we now all take for granted on bank credit cards that have largely replaced the use of cheques. It is the opaque strip on the reverse, which conceals a lot of magnetic data, including the cheque number, bank sorting code, and the name and number of the account holder. That was what Williams claimed to have invented and copyrighted when he printed his first cheque-like bills of exchange in 1968, reinforcing the point on his pioneering Welsh pound note in 1969. He said his "black patch" magnetic system could comfortably contain up to 200 characters compared with only 30 on the prevailing E-13B numeric system – which he also claimed to be his.

Against that background he hoped to find an American lawyer who would take on his fight in the United States for no fee, but a share of the compensation when they won the case. He submitted an advertisement for publication in the November 1979 issue of the *American Bar Association Journal,* which had a printed circulation of 230,000. Under the heading of "$20,000,000,000", the submitted copy for his intended advertisement said:

"That is estimated as a reasonable share of the profits of the banks of the USA who, since about 1960, have used and are using one of the several systems of magnetic check encoding systems invented by Richard Williams in 1954, and which is protected by his copyright. Neither the banks concerned nor their equipment suppliers have any patent or prior copyright.

"Cwmni y Ddafad Ddu Gymreig Ltd., the former Chief Treasury of Wales Ltd. (the Vendor), who by a deed of transfer of 29 June 1971, obtained the rights of Computer Consultants Ltd. and Richard Hugh Williams (the original inventor) OFFER American lawyers and their clients the opportunity to purchase claims for the INFRINGEMENT of those rights against not more than twenty separate and individual banks of their choice, in each package agreement, all to be in one State in each instance, on payment of ONE DOLLAR, such claims to be prosecuted by them or any company they may name or may incorporate in the USA for that purpose. This offer is subject to a mutual written agreement on certain relevant conditions, e.g. the cost of depositions, attendance of witnesses, preparation of the Deed of Transfer, etc.

"Summarised detailed information will be given, upon request accompanied by $18,25 to cover costs, to bona fide applicants who wish to take advantage of this offer. The Vendor has an account, No. 112075-1, opened in 1969, with the Michigan National Bank, Cassopolis, Michigan, who are to be exempt from this claim.

"Less than 1,000 assignments will be made, and to avoid duplication and delays, indication of the names of the banks to be sued, and their main office addresses, should be given at an early stage. The suggested individual claim figure for each bank should be $1-million."

To the dismay of Richard Williams, who hoped for dramatic test cases in a land that thrives on speculative "no cure, no pay" litigation, the American Bar Association refused to publish his advertisement. They never gave a reason, and Williams declared them to be "a lot of wimps". They were clearly not of the stuff of which he was made, as demonstrated in his single-handed ten-year war against the British financial Establishment.

Chapter 11
Man on the Moon

Richard Williams founded Computer Consultants Ltd. in 1957, with his wife as the only other director. He claimed to be Europe's first such consultant, and before long was advising clients from Sweden in the north to a NATO anti-submarine base in Italy. He wrote and published a flow of books on the subject and by 1970 his status was such that he could assemble ten of the world's greatest brains in the computer business to address a two-day summer school, at his home town of Llandudno – where he simultaneously staged a Man on the Moon Exhibition and a Computer Pioneers Exhibition.

For his Man on the Moon display, for which he hired the local Territorial Army Drill Hall, he managed to persuade America's National Aeronautics and Space Administration to lend him the Apollo 12 space capsule computer that had controlled the second landing on the moon. *"This is the computer that handled the mission whilst we were in orbit around the moon, landing on the moon and returning from the moon,"* confirmed a NASA spokesman to the author, while an armoured car and escort waited in vain for its arrival at Manchester airport.

Richard Williams called in Scotland Yard who traced its arrival at London Airport, by BOAC, on 17 June. Instead of being put on a plane for Manchester it disappeared, but two days later the police found it in a bonded warehouse in London. Responding to the news, Williams said: *"I hope Britain can eventually manage to deliver from London to Wales something which the Americans were able to send to the Moon and back! On the other hand, perhaps London thinks Wales is on the Moon."* Although weighing only 60-lbs, the errant computer was delivered to Llandudno by escorted lorry, to become the centrepiece of a remarkable display. The Computer Pioneers Exhibition, at the Winter Gardens ballroom, on the other side of town, included parts of Charles Babbage's 19th century Analytical Engine, borrowed from the London Science Museum.

People arriving at Llandudno Pier that day saw an impressive banner proclaiming: *"World computer pioneers, who made the past and will shape the future."* Anyone minded to pay the 10s entrance fee to the conference would have discovered that such computer giants as Grace Hopper, J.Presper Eckert, Konrad Zuse and Robert Zagrodnick had been assembled.

Presper Eckert, vice-president of Sperry Rand Corporation's UNIVAC Division, was the co-inventor of the world's first all-electronic computer, in 1946. It weighed 30 tons and had to be partially rewired for every new problem, but within two hours it could provide the answer to a problem that would otherwise have taken a year to solve.

Konrad Zuse, whose computer development work began in Nazi Germany, designed the Z3 computer used to solve the engineering problems for the V1 flying bombs that rained down on London towards the end of World War Two.

Robert Zagrodnick, the Apollo computer programme manager at NASA, had travelled to Llandudno for the Man on the Moon Exhibition and to present five film shows on the Apollo 11, 12 and 13 space flights. He was persuaded to speak as one of the "computer pioneers" as a late substitute for Bruno Leclerc, head of the French team that developed the Gamma 3 business-orientated electronic calculator in 1952. He cancelled his Llandudno engagement, saying he had to go to the United States for company merger talks.

Most colourful of all the speakers was 64-years-old Dr. Grace Hopper, who turned up wearing the uniform of a commander in the U.S. Navy, with a sea of medal ribbons across her chest. During her young naval reserve days, seconded to Sperry Rand, she was put to work on America's first computer – later recalling it was 51-ft long, 8-ft high, and 6-ft deep. In those days computer programmers had to type laborious instructions in symbols known as machine code. Grace Hopper realised that before computers could become standard equipment a simpler program-ming language would need to be devised. From that she developed the Common Business-orientated Language, known as COBOL, which became universal.

In between the conference sessions Commander Hopper was to be seen gleefully using her mathematical brain to defeat the fruit machines on the Pier, successfully harvesting pennies which she gave to the nearest child. Re-entering the hall she proclaimed: *"There are much better computers out there, and they pay real money!"*

She told the Llandudno conference she wanted to live until she was 94, so that she could enjoy the "splendid parties" on the last day of 1999. *"Then perhaps I will retire to a mountain top, with a computer, and send messages to everyone telling them where they are going wrong,"* she said. Grace Hopper was a rear-admiral when she died in January 1992 – and seven years later the world lived in fear of Hopper's Millennium Bug, for which governments issued special literature on how to cope after 1 January 2000. Despite her wish to see out 1999 she had made no provision in her COBOL programme for anything other than a two-digit recognition of years. Thus, on the first day of the present millennium, many older computers and such equipment as video recorders reverted to 1900.

Unfortunately for Richard Williams no member of the public was persuaded to pay ten-shillings to see and hear this galaxy of the good and the great of the computer world. He had hired the 2,000-seat Pier Pavilion for the event but at the last minute switched it to the adjoining Caesar's Palace, normally a nightclub. As *Dataweek* reported: *"The Computer Pioneers' conference, planned as a gigantic data processing convention...crashed when less than fifty people arrived, including ten speakers and a dozen journalists."* The rest were exhibitors and Williams's friends and relations.

"*It was a sad commentary on the conference that a nearby puppet show, called Professor Codman's Wooden-headed Follies, was daily drawing larger crowds than Eckert, Zuse, Hopper and other speakers,*" added *Dataweek*.

Once again Richard Williams was a man before his time, and in December 1971 a winding up order for Computer Consultants Ltd. was made by Swansea Official Receiver. The logo of Computer Consultants Ltd. lives on in note collectors' albums, as part of the design of all Richard Williams's notes printed under the name of Prif Trysorfa Cymru Limited – the Chief Treasury of Wales.

I'd Like To Help You

Out ...

Which way did you come in?

**RICHARD WILLIAMS & PARTNERS
COMPUTER SPECIALISTS**

P.O. BOX NO. 8, LLANDUDNO, WALES, GREAT BRITAIN.

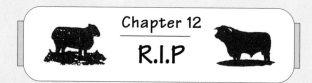
After a long and painful illness Richard Hugh Williams died in November 1988, aged 73, and was cremated at Colwyn Bay. Readers who did not know him might be surprised to learn that his notoriously robust contest with the privileged power of bankers, lawyers, civil servants and Government ministers, was conducted by a genial, good-humoured, soft-spoken, friendly character, whose activities amused himself as much as anyone else. He died bankrupt but genuinely believing the banks of the world owed him countless million of pounds, for the international adoption of both the distinctive numeric information along the bottom of all our cheques and what has now become the familiar opaque strip concealing lots of electronic data on our credit cards. He believed himself to be the inventor of both systems, and always maintained that no evidence to the contrary had ever been produced during the many years of costly litigation he always lost.

The Welsh Pound was conceived almost by accident, intended as a one-off by-product to emphasise his other activities. Once born, it was rapidly developed and nurtured during discussions with the author, whose role of political journalist with a deep interest in history, and daily access to Richard Williams's amusing correspondence, helped shape the extraordinary saga of the man who printed his own money. Although widely interpreted as a Nationalist gesture (with several journals actually saying so in print), that was never the intention. Patriotic yes, but never politically Nationalist. Towards the end of his life Richard Williams said Wales would soon forget his David and Goliath fight for justice, but his pioneering Welsh pound notes had been distributed across the world and would keep turning up for evermore, to puzzle collectors and feed the imagination of generations yet unborn.

He had been dead six-and-a-half years when, in April 1995, his cry for Welsh paper money was taken up by Gwynedd County Council's bilingual sub-committee – but without any reference to Richard Williams. The committee asked the Bank of England to consider issuing bilingual notes that would raise the profile of the Welsh language. A precedent had already been established, noted the committee, by the Royal Mint's 1985 issue of a £1 coin bearing the words *Pleidiol wyf i'm gwlad*.

Wales still awaits such official implementation of Richard Williams's Welsh paper money dream. If he were still alive there would certainly now be a Welsh Euro, to confuse the citizens of the European Community who are still mourning the demise of the *franc* (dating from 1795), *guilder* (1816), *drachma* (1833), *markka* (1860), *lira* (1861), *peseta* (1869), *mark* (1873), *krone* (1873), *escudo*

(1910) and *schilling* (1924), with other currencies destined to follow in the enlarged EC. Only the Irish seemed happy to see the last of their *punt,* perhaps because it was merely a Gaelic translation of the English pound the republic inherited in 1921.

Richard Williams 1915-1988

Llanrwst branch of the Midland Bank where Richard Williams spent the early years of his career.

Index

A celebration of Welsh Heritage

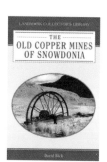

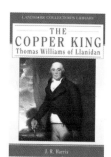

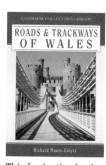

The miners' path to the summit of Snowdon is a reminder of the old mines that were once worked amid the magnificent scenery of Snowdonia. The history of nearly 50 mines is explored and includes details of some of the personalities.
ISBN 1 84306 075 2
Price £ 9.95 160 pages paper back

The Copper King records the spectacular rise to fame and fortune of Thomas Williams during the 18th century.
ISBN 1 84306 092 2
Price £19.95 192 pages hard back

This title provides the reader with an insight into all aspects of this town including its claims to fame, wartime memories and its tradition of entertainment.
ISBN 1 84306 048 5
Price £15.95 144 pages hard back

This fascinating book looks at the roads and trackways of Wales from Roman times through to the development of the turnpike system. The author is Professor of Agrarian History at the University of Wales.
ISBN 1 84306 019 1
Price £22.50 192 pages hard back

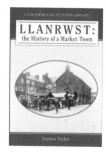

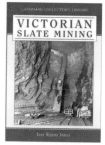

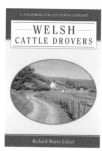

This book traces the rise of this market town from its early beginnings to the end of the 19th century. There are over 70 black and white photographs revealing the towns rich heritage.
ISBN 1 84603 070 1
Price £14.95 112 pages hard back

Victorian Slate Mining provides a social commentary and photographic record of the Welsh slate mining industry. It focuses on the Llechwedd and Blaenau Ffestiniog mines.
ISBN 1 84306 073 6
Price £15.95 144 pages hard back

Welsh Cattle Drovers gives an insight into how the cattle drovers operated between Wales and England; how towns developed along the drovers' roads and how one drover set up the Black Ox Bank now owned by Lloyds bank!
ISBN 1 84306 021 3
Price £22.50 192 pages hard back

These books make a useful addition to any collection for those who want to learn more about Wales and its rich culture and history. They also represent an ideal opportunity to pass on memories to children and grandchildren of how their surroundings have developed over the years.

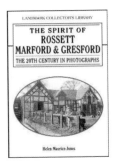
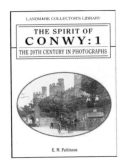
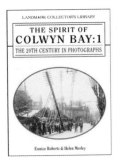